T

Jennie Wade Story

A True and Complete Account of the
Only Civilian Killed During the Battle of Gettysburg

by
Cindy L. Small

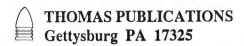

THOMAS PUBLICATIONS
Gettysburg PA 17325

Mary Virginia Wade, about 1861. The only civilian killed during the Battle of Gettysburg.

Contents

Dedication

To everyone who, at some time in their lives, felt their story was misunderstood, and wished that someone would make the effort to set the record straight.

Acknowledgements

The first acknowledgement must be of Gregory A. Coco. No one could have been more generous with advice about *The Jennie Wade Story*. A tireless consultant to this publication, he proved that we can truly be partners in *everything* we do.

Dean S. Thomas provided, with no small pains, the patience, enthusiasm, sound judgment and expertise needed to finalize this project.

Most frequently visited was the Adams County Historical Society, under the scholarly direction of Dr. Charles H. Glatfelter, who settled some perplexing mysteries and painstakingly answered my many questions. Also at this location I received the notable assistance of Elwood W. Christ who facilitated the research for a special building study of historic structures in Gettysburg; and Cheryl Snyder, whose prompt and thorough direction toward endless sources, was much appreciated.

William A. Frassanito, a noted Civil War historian and author, went over the manuscript and offered many helpful comments and suggestions.

William A. Cole, of Eastern National Park and Monument Association, deserves my sincere thanks for his encouragement of and suggestion for the existence of this book. This project began because of his realization that this publication should be made available to all people interested in the Battle of Gettysburg. And thank you, Bill, for the title.

Deah Schwarzenbach Bruhn and Kenneth Wade Schwarzenbach are worthy of my deep appreciation for their willingness to release much family information that was not possibly attainable elsewhere. Their long-distance communications were invaluable.

To four very gifted people, a debt is due. Edward F. Guy, Jr.; Debra A. Novotny; Daniel E. Fuhrman; and Elizabeth Richwine generously contributed their artistic talents to add the word "quality" to this publication.

Kathleen Georg Harrison, Robert H. Prosperi, and Karen L. Finley, all of Gettysburg National Military Park, directed me toward much useful information regarding civilian accounts and were very thorough in exhausting all research possibilities.

Walter L. Powell, Ph.D., Mark V. Nesbitt, Fred W. Hawthorne, Rebecca A. Lyons, James Clouse and Wayne Motts, all, who upon every encounter, touched me by their openness and willingness to share their leads, information, research files, conclusions, and their enthusiasm. Their matchless generosity will be forever remembered.

Leatrice M. Kemp of the Rochester Museum & Science Center, Walt Lane of Lane Studio in Gettysburg, the Carnegie Library of Pittsburgh, and Thomas R. Thompson of the Christian C. Sanderson Museum in Chadds Ford, Pennsylvania, deserve my thanks for their complete cooperation and assistance in procuring the numerous photographs in this book.

Myrtle Hankey and Merlin and Lucy Coco delighted me by informing me of some valuable information and photographs at a time when I needed the boost you can only get from uncovering an unexpected discovery.

The charitable offer by Philip B. Ennis to drive the many miles to Chadds Ford for two important photographs was exceedingly generous as it saved me some precious time.

Thank you all for making this a chapter in my life that I will always remember.

Foreword

Each year over a million visitors come to see the historic town and battlefield of Gettysburg. They hear the story of how two great armies grappled with each other for three hot July days in 1863. Names such as George G. Meade, Robert E. Lee, John F. Reynolds, James Longstreet, Strong Vincent and Lewis Armistead echo from the likes of battlefield guides, commercial audio tapes and bus tour recordings.

In all of this, only one woman's name is ever mentioned - Mary Virginia "Jennie" Wade. Jennie was the only Gettysburg civilian to be killed outright during the battle. In 20th Century wars, civilian deaths are very common, but during the Civil War citizens were usually unmolested if they were able to stay out of harm's way. However, on July 3 Jennie was kneading dough for biscuits at her sister's home on Baltimore Street when she was killed instantly as a bullet passed through two wooden doors and struck her heart. That, unfortunately, is usually all visitors hear about this "Gettysburg Maid" - a mere sentence or two.

Now, with this book, *The Jennie Wade Story, A True and Complete Account of the Only Civilian Killed During the Battle of Gettysburg*, a visitor seeking more of her story may now be satisfied. The author has investigated as many sources as possible to write the full saga of Jennie's life, death and all three burials.

I thank Cindy Small for giving Mary Virginia Wade more than a footnote in history, as her untimely sacrifice demands that a true and complete narrative be told!

Debra A. Novotny
Gettysburg, PA
April 19, 1991

In that year of the great battle, the year and the battle the old-timers would talk about for generations to come, the cold winds and snows of winter had finally given way to spring, and spring to warm, sultry summer. The land was rich and beautiful and for the people who lived in Adams County, Pennsylvania life was good. It was in fact, almost as good as it could get in the United States of America in 1863, — except, of course, for the War.

Naturally, the war was on the minds of almost everyone in those days. The 20,000 or so citizens of the county were used to it; after all, the fighting now was into its third year, and no one really knew when it would end. The inhabitants, although quite far from the seat of war, had their share of suffering. Many of their sons, husbands, brothers and friends were as yet under arms in various Federal armies, while not a few had even joined the Southern Army. There had been deaths also. In Gettysburg and in the towns and villages which surrounded it, at Littlestown, and Bendersville, and out near New Chester, families with German and Scotch-Irish surnames sadly mourned soldier relatives dead by disease or from Confederate bullets. But what seemed even worse for the sturdy farmers and thrifty shopkeepers was the constant *threat* of invasion. From children on up, all well knew that the Maryland border was barely ten miles south of Gettysburg. Why, just last October during the crisp autumn of 1862, Rebel cavalry had come raiding up along the South Mountains into Franklin County, a scant twenty miles westward. A band of these marauders had boldly scavenged eastward into Adams County, stealing all they could lay hands on and scaring the wits out of everyone they encountered and many they didn't. The losses were not severe, and really no one got hurt, but it was still the *idea* that at any moment a Confederate enemy force, an entire army, might slip over from Virginia, cover the few gentle miles through tiny Maryland, and Great Gods, they'd be right on the doorsteps, and among the fertile, lush fields of the county.

The truth was, that no clear-minded citizen slept well during those scares. All it took these days was a good rumor to have country people and townsfolk alike rushing to hide their worldly possessions while shooing valuable livestock into dense woods and secret mountain coves.

The town of Gettysburg was a particular case in point. You see, it had banks and the railroad, and warehouses and a few fair-sized stores. The 2,000-odd populace just knew that the Rebs, if they came North again, would surely pay the borough a "friendly" visit. But there were people too who laughed at these so far unfounded fears and brushed off the rumors, and said there's work to be done and money to be made, so they ignored the whispers on the wind, and the ominous rumblings that rent the heavy summer air like black storm clouds rolling in from the west.

The reader, more than a century later, will certainly know the rest of the story. In that memorable June of eighteen hundred and sixty-three, General Robert E. Lee's Confederate Army of Northern Virginia, 75,000 strong, with its miles of infantry, artillery, cavalry and thousands of horses, wagons and cannon, did indeed invade the Commonwealth of Pennsylvania, a prominent and significant part of the United States of America. There, on the first three days of July, at the crossroads town of Gettysburg, an unplanned collision with General George G. Meade's powerful Army of the Potomac, resulted in the greatest battle ever fought on American soil. In the course of that titanic struggle, more than 51,000 men were killed, wounded or reported missing in action. Ironically, or miraculously, during those days and nights of grim and intense combat, only one civilian was killed. Her name was Mary Virginia Wade. The tragic circumstances surrounding her death have always been one of the most interesting and fascinating aspects of the battle.

This is her true and complete story.

Chapter 1

"...And the story hear of poor Jennie Wade,
The noble name of the Gettysburg maid..."[1]

Mary Virginia Wade was born in Gettysburg, Adams County, Pennsylvania, to a father of English descent and a mother whose ancestors were German. Her father, James Wade, Sr., was born in James City, Virginia to Thomas Wade and Elizabeth Mills on August 9, 1814. Her mother, Mary Ann Filby Wade, was born in 1820, in York, Pennsylvania, the first child of Samuel Filby and Elizabeth Maria de Groff. James and Mary were married on April 15, 1840 and started a family fifteen months later when their daughter, Georgeana or "Georgia" was born on July 4. Two years later, Mary Virginia arrived into the world on a beautiful May 21 in 1843. The couple's firstborn son, John James joined the family on March 13, 1846, followed by Martha Margaret on May 9, 1849, who died as an infant just four months later on September 16. After two years, Samuel Swan was born on August 6, 1851, who, as a three-year-old, was delighted to get a baby brother, Harry Marion on February 4, 1855. All of the Wade children were christened in the local Trinity Reformed Church. Mary Virginia was baptized there on January 1, 1845 by Reverend Samuel Gutelius and nineteen years later she was confirmed and united with the St. James Lutheran Church which stood on York Street in the village of her birth.[2]

Her birthplace, built some time between 1814 and 1820, was a small clapboard house at the crest of a low hill on Baltimore Street in Gettysburg. While renting that house from John Pfoutz, the Wade family lived in the northern half as James Wade used the southern side for his tailoring shop.[3]

As a child, Mary Virginia attended the local schools while she continued to earn money to help support her family by doing housework and sewing within her father's tailoring trade. When she grew to be a young girl, her schoolmates often called her "Gin" or "Ginnie" by reason of her middle name. The title "Jennie" was a subsequent newspaper inaccuracy which has persisted even within her own family. Mary Virginia's younger friends may have nicknamed her "Ginnie" but as the years went by she was referred to as "Jennie" by even her mother, her brothers and sister and by her closest male friend.[4]

Georgia Wade, 20; Maria Comfort, 48; and Mary Virginia Wade, 18 in 1861. Maria Comfort, Georgia's friend, lived with her husband, Henry, and her son, Charles, on Baltimore Street across from Jennie's birthplace and just 200 yards from the Wade family's Breckenridge Street home.

When James Wade, Sr.'s health failed in the early 1850s, Mary Wade and her daughters began to work as seamstresses so that they could retain ownership of the neat, rectangular house they had built which was one of the first houses constructed on Breckenridge Street. This was the dwelling they called home when two vast armies invaded their peaceful town of 2,400 inhabitants in 1863.[5]

The social status of the Wade family was ofttimes a sensitive subject in the hamlet, due mostly to troubles caused by Jennie's father. According to the September 2, 1850 issue of the Adams *Sentinel* James Wade, Sr. was arrested for taking $300 of Samuel Durboraw's money which had "dropped from his pocket whilst engaged in some business" in Gettysburg. The article continued, stating, "Suspicion was excited against James Wade (tailor)...who had gone into Maryland and was making a 'flourish' there. He was followed by Mr. Durboraw, and Constable Weaver, and arrested in Washington City, and about $240, identified as a portion of the lost money, found in his possession." It should be noted that it was quite improper in times such as this to play "finders-keepers" - it was imperative for the finder to place an advertisement in the newspaper and ask for proof of ownership. A week later, the same paper recorded that Wade was extradited from Washington, D.C. and indicted for, "larceny in the case of the missing money of Samuel Durboraw at Gettysburg" by Justice Joel B. Danner. On November 25, the publication claimed that Wade had been convicted of larceny and sentenced to two years of solitary confinement at Eastern Penitentiary in Philadelphia.[6]

James Wade's conduct must not have improved in the ensuing years, for in January of 1852, Mary Wade petitioned the Adams County Court of Common Pleas to have her husband declared "very insane" and he was committed to the Adams County Alms House or "Poor House" which stood just north of Gettysburg. This turn of events left Mrs. Wade and her young daughters with the responsibility of supporting their seemingly endless financial woes.[7]

Ten years later in 1862, Georgia wed John Louis McClellan of Gettysburg on April 15, which was also her parents' wedding anniversary. Born on April 7, 1838 to unmarried Colonel John Joseph Henry McClellan and Mary Blakely, Louis McClellan spent his youthful days playing in the hallways, rooms, and kitchen where he lived at the McClellan Hotel, which had been in his family since 1808. He was educated in the public school and then attended Pennsylvania College in Gettysburg until the outbreak of the Civil War, when he responded to President Abraham Lincoln's first call for volunteers. John Louis enlisted in the 2nd Pennsylvania Infantry Regiment and between periods of service he wed Georgia, standing proud and tall in his new military uniform. Although Louis soon headed back to camp, newly married Georgia moved into a rented northern half of a double house on south Baltimore Street near Cemetery Hill. This marriage burdened nineteen-year-old Jennie with helping her mother maintain the household as she became her main support in sustaining a home for themselves and for her brothers.[8]

Georgia Wade McClellan. Born July 4, 1841. On her 22nd birthday, she would stand at the muddy, gaping grave of her sister, Jennie, who was killed one day before.

Chapter 2

*"...The quiet village o'er hill and glen
Was stirred by the sound of marching men..."*

In the winter of 1861-62 with the Civil War now seven months old, the 10th New York Cavalry Regiment, known as "The Porter Guards," was ordered to Gettysburg where it was stationed for three months. The New Yorkers spent those long wintry days drilling and perfecting the use of sabers and small arms for they had been sent to protect the state's borders against any possible Southern intrusion. From time to time Mary Wade and her daughters repaired uniforms and performed other similar services for these soldiers. The Wade women were highly respected by the New York men who described them as kindly and hospitable. Occasionally, Jennie invited the visiting troopers to attend services at St. James Lutheran Church.[9]

Even with so much to occupy her time, these were lonely days for Jennie, who was longing to see a particular young man, Johnston Hastings "Jack" Skelly, Jr., who was miles away fighting in the Union Army with the 8th Corps in Virginia.

In the years prior to the Civil War, Jennie and Jack played together with other school children in the streets, fields and woods around Gettysburg. It seems that the carefree friendship they had developed grew into one of long serious talks in which they exchanged their innermost dreams for the future. Their friendship, it was said, blossomed into what could have been called love. But war has a way of separating those in love and Jack Skelly bade Jennie farewell and shouldered a musket to defend the Union which left her to the task of praying for his safe return. She treasured every letter he wrote, but in her favorite correspondence he renewed his vows of loyalty to the Union and to her, a message she so cherished that she carried it in her dress next to her heart.[10]

Some of Skelly's boyhood friends moved away, seeking adventure or employment, only to be reunited when all the available men were gathering for military service. About seven years before the Battle of Gettysburg, in 1856, C. William Hoffman, owner of a Gettysburg carriage shop moved his business to Shepherdstown, Virginia, now West Virginia. A number of his

Johnston Hastings Skelly, Jr. In April of 1861 he was mustered into Co. E, 2nd PA Volunteer Infantry.

Gettysburg workmen went with him, among them, John Wesley Culp, who sewed the upholstery, and Charles Edwin Skelly, the older brother of Jack Skelly. Jack had no reason to leave Gettysburg with the Hoffman employees as he was a stonemason and granite cutter by trade, and unlike his father who was a tailor, he was almost always employed.[11]

While living in Virginia, Wesley Culp, as he was generally known, joined the Southern army, an action that his beloved hometown and even his own brother never understood nor really forgave him. This following explanation, which may have been accepted by those who knew Wesley intimately, could provide a partial answer. In Shepherdstown there was a social and military organization that had existed prior to the Civil War called the Hamtramck Guards, named for a resident, Colonel J.F. Hamtramck, a veteran of the War with Mexico. Wesley Culp, who liked the military, promptly joined the "Guards." Were his sympathies Southern? No one in Gettysburg really ever knew. But it was advantageous for him to join the local military company because it whiled away the tedium of life for this young man in a strange community and it gave him the opportunity to meet many acquaintances and gain some good friends.[12]

When the tragic War Between the States began in 1861, the little coterie of Gettysburg workmen in Shepherdstown prepared to return home. "Get ready, Wes," his companions said to him, "we're going North." "No,"

14

replied Wesley Culp, determinedly, "I am going to stay here, come what may," and stay he did while Edwin Skelly and the others sorrowfully bade him goodbye. The Hamtramck Guards were later enrolled as Company B of the Second Virginia Infantry Regiment, which would become part of the famed "Stonewall" Brigade, a unit Wesley would serve in through all of its campaigns until that fateful summer of 1863.[13]

Meanwhile, in the Northern states the call to arms was quickly answered by the men of quiet, rural Gettysburg. When the Second Pennsylvania Volunteers was mustered in on April 29, 1861, in the ranks of Company E stood Corporal William E. Culp, Wesley's brother, as well as Private Johnston H. Skelly.

The Skellys firmly supported the United States, and Jack, then twenty years old, was one of the first to enlist. "My country needs me, mother," he said, "May I go?" "Yes, my boy," she answered, "and may God bless and keep you." So Jack Skelly went off to war with the Second Pennsylvania, where speculation was always rife as to what had become of their friend, John Wesley Culp.

The three months' service of these Pennsylvania troops in the initial year of the Civil War was a bloodless one. In July the Battle of Bull Run was fought, which gave an early victory to the South and inspired President Lincoln and unified the North more completely than a victory would have done. "Give me 300,000 men for three years" called Father Abraham, in his

John Wesley Culp. A Gettysburg boy in the Confederate army, he would die on his cousin's farm.

distress. "We'll give our quota," replied loyal Gettysburg, and it did. Most of the boys of Company E, Second Pennsylvania later reenlisted into Company F of the Eighty-seventh Pennsylvania Volunteer Infantry, including Jack Skelly, now a corporal. New recruits also joined; Charles Edwin Skelly, William T. Ziegler and William "Billy" Holtzworth. William Culp was promoted first sergeant and later became an officer and quartermaster of that regiment. All were old acquaintances of Wesley Culp. Johnston H. Skelly, Sr., not to be outdone by his sons, enlisted and served in Company K, 101st Pennsylvania Volunteer Infantry, a company partially recruited in the Gettysburg area.[14]

General Robert E. Lee's second invasion of the North began in early June, 1863, and one portion of his Confederate Army of Northern Virginia marched through Winchester, Virginia where they captured the town and tons of U.S. supplies, fighting a minor engagement in the process. After the capture, Wesley Culp, who was present with his regiment, recognized some of his childhood friends who had been taken prisoner in what was called the battle of Carter's Woods. Ironically, both Wesley and William Culp participated in that battle, on opposite sides. William was with the defenders of Winchester while Wesley was with the attacking rebels. Truly, brother had fought against brother.[15]

On Monday, June 15, many of General Robert H. Milroy's Federal troops were surrounded in the fighting in Carter's Woods. William Culp escaped, but others from Gettysburg were captured, among them were Corporal Skelly and Sergeants Ziegler and Holtzworth. During the action Skelly was called upon to surrender. He and several other men attempted to flee. Shots rang out and Skelly was struck in the upper arm with a Minie' ball.[16]

When the victorious force, Johnson's Division of Ewell's Corps, passed by in pursuit, a familiar voice greeted Sergeant Holtzworth who was one of the unfortunate prisoners standing by the wayside. It was his friend, Wesley Culp, who greeted him with a sympathetic "hello." When Wesley offered to help him just as if they were not enemies, Holtzworth immediately solicited medical aid for his comrade, Jack Skelly. Wesley was saddened to learn that such bad luck had overtaken his schoolmate and he instantly took the actions necessary to have Skelly moved to a field hospital in the town.[17]

Some time later Wesley visited Jack in the Taylor House Hospital in Winchester where Skelly gave him a message "in case he got to Gettysburg," referring to the fact that the Confederate army was possibly enroute to Pennsylvania as part of its invasion plans. It has always been believed by the families that the message was for Skelly's sweetheart, Jennie Wade, but others thought Skelly breathed only a dying sentiment to his beloved mother. When Wesley left Jack that day, it was the last time they would ever meet.[18]

Seventy miles northeastward, early summer was upon the rolling fertile fields and woods, and word of the approaching Rebel army would soon reach the tranquil inhabitants of Gettysburg. In these troubled times, Jennie Wade, notwithstanding her father's Southern heritage, never faltered in her feelings of patriotism. She had been surrounded most of her life by family members who willingly served in the military of the United States of America. As an example, her great-grandfather, Colonel Chidley Wade, was killed during the American Revolution and was among the casualties of nearly 1,000 men at the Battle of Brandywine on September 11, 1777. Her grandfather, Thomas Wade, aide de camp to General Marquis de Lafayette, was wounded at the same battle. And just prior to the Mexican War, Jennie's father was elected a captain in the 80th Pennsylvania militia, being commissioned by Governor David R. Porter on August 3, 1842. More recently, in 1861, her sister's husband, J. Louis McClellan, had answered Lincoln's first call for volunteers and after his ninety-day term expired he reenlisted with the 165th Pennsylvania Volunteers, a nine-month regiment and would serve until July, 1863.[19]

During the everchanging events of that year, Jennie heard most of the frightening rumors spread by the neighbors and relatives around her. But, she, like most residents, never considered fleeing the town.

Georgia's neighbor, Lydia Catherine Ziegler recalled later that "the spring and summer of '63 were days in which the citizens of our quiet village were much disturbed." Thirty-year-old Sarah M. Broadhead wrote in her diary that real alarm was not felt until June 15 when a telegram came from Governor Andrew W. Curtin advising Gettysburg citizens to move their stores to more secure places as quickly as possible. On June 20 messages arrived from General Darius N. Couch, Commander of the Department of the Susquehanna, that residents should see to their own protection, which was sufficiently terrifying enough to incite a meeting at the Court House for "placing the county in a state of military organization as would be deemed most advisable."[20]

The Gettysburg *Compiler* of June 22, 1863 reprinted a Baltimore *Sun* article which reported 2,000 Southern troops occupying Chambersburg but that "excitement was subsiding." On the other hand, the Adams *Sentinel*, the town's second newspaper, on the same day thought it possible "that a great battle will be fought...a collision is almost certain."

Throughout the latter part of that fateful month, Adams Countians eagerly followed newspaper accounts and listened to any and all rumors with increasing apprehension.

Chapter 3

"...And Jennie listened, with bated breath,
To the direful tocsin of war and death,
For Lee with his dreadful hosts had come
To invade her quiet and happy home..."

On June 26 the Gettysburg community came face-to-face with their worst fears.

According to Robert F. McClean, 18, of Gettysburg, Confederate General Jubal A. Early's men triumphantly entered the town on that day via Chambersburg Street, the officers brandishing swords and the troops firing their guns into the air. To ten-year-old Gates D. Fahnestock, who in the safety of his home peered out through the slatted shutters, the spectacle was to be enjoyed "as they would a wild west show."[21]

But to Jennie Wade, the arrival of the Rebels spelled the advent of many ominous events within her family which would manifest themselves during the course of that unforgettable day and long afterwards.

On that momentous Friday, her mother was staying at Georgia's house on Baltimore Street, caring for her daughter who had given birth to her first child, Louis Kenneth, with the assistance of a doctor who had remained in the town. The baby was born at about two thirty - just one hour before the Southerners marched into Gettysburg. This placed Jennie accountable for sustaining the family home on Breckenridge Street, which was located a little over five hundred yards northward toward the village.[22]

One of Jennie's most important tasks was to care for Isaac Brinkerhoff, a boarder the Wades had taken in to earn extra money to make ends meet. Six-year-old Isaac was a crippled boy whose mother worked away from home during the week, and he could not care for himself because he was unable to walk. Looking after Isaac and her little brother Harry, age eight, was very time-consuming for Jennie, especially while she also carried the responsibilities of many other jobs.

Despite all of this, Jennie put these duties aside when an older brother called upon her to help him prepare to enter the Union Army. Jennie's brother, John, nicknamed "Jack," was yet another family member who was intensely devoted to his country and its cause. Jack, who was seventeen,

Louis Kenneth McClellan. The "youngest veteran of the Battle of Gettysburg."

had enlisted in Company B of the 21st Pennsylvania Cavalry Regiment on June 23, 1863, and had been assigned duty as bugler. He was very small for his age, a mere five feet three inches, and when his uniform was issued it was found to be about two sizes too large. Using her talents as a seamstress, Jennie began at once to refit the garments.[23]

The 21st Pennsylvania Cavalry, which had been ordered to southern Pennsylvania for scouting duty because of the invasion, happened to leave Gettysburg on June 26 by the York Road just a few hours prior to the Confederates' grand entrance into town from the opposite direction. Bugler Wade was not ready to depart with the others, but later, in his newly altered uniform, hurriedly rode his horse out of town alone, endeavoring to catch up with his comrades. Their wave goodbye, the clattering hooves, the dusty street, were all a final memory, for this sister and brother would never cross paths again.

A third sibling, twelve-year-old Samuel, lived with and worked as a delivery boy for James Pierce, a butcher at the end of Breckenridge Street. Sam was a member of the "Gettysburg Zouaves," a semi-military organization. Immediately after the Rebels rode into Gettysburg, they began to collect the serviceable horses of the village. Samuel was instructed by Mr. Pierce to take this family's favorite horse - an iron grey animal of some value - and ride out of town along the Baltimore Pike to safety. With no hesitation, the lad mounted the animal and rode a short distance out on the main street toward the turnpike when he was overtaken by enemy soldiers who led him back to town and placed him under arrest.[24]

At that moment, Jennie was near the corner of Breckenridge and

Baltimore Streets and quickly learned that her brother was being held captive. She approached his captors and pleaded with them to release young Samuel. When she failed to convince them to do so, she ran directly to the McClellan residence where her mother was still tending to Georgia. Not wishing to disturb her sister, Jennie called her mother out of the house to explain the circumstances of Samuel's arrest. Mrs. Wade went to the Town Square or "Diamond" as it was known in the 1860s, and appeared before General Early at about four o'clock in the afternoon where she was successful in securing the release of her son. The horse, however, was retained by the Southern Army. Samuel spent the remainder of the battle safely in the cellar at James Pierce's home.[25]

Friday, June 26, 1863 had been quite a day for Jennie Wade as well as the other people of Gettysburg. First, there was the birth of her sister's child, then the rush to repair her brother's oversized uniform in time for him to ride off with his command, the unexpected arrival of Confederate troops, the arrest of Samuel, the absence of her mother from their home, and of course, the ever-present fear of what the next few dreaded days might bring.

The McClellan House. The north side shows many battle scars.

Chapter 4

"...Soon ominous sounds from near and far
Proclaimed the tiding of terrible war... "

Early's Division departed from Gettysburg the next morning. The townspeople's brief experience under enemy occupation had reminded them of their vulnerable location and provided a hint of what they might possibly experience on a larger scale in the not-too-distant future. Some were sufficiently alarmed that they immediately took measures to protect their property against a return of the invaders.

As examples, Charles Will and his son, John C. Will, proprietors of the Globe Hotel, moved a store of foodstuffs such as sugar, hams, potatoes and other groceries to the loft of their York Street hostelry. Charles Will even went so far as to bury a supply of liquor in his garden under a row of young cabbage plants. James F. Fahnestock leased an entire freight car in which he shipped his stock of goods to Philadelphia. Similarly, Leonard H. Gardner noted that as far away as York Springs "horses were being hid in the woods or hurried off to the river."[26]

The *Compiler* newspaper of Monday, June 29 gave readers new cause for their mounting fears when it reported that a force of 13,000 Southerners with twenty-three cannon and a long wagon train were encamped less than five miles northeast in the village of Mummasburg. And all through that calm, warm night the people of Gettysburg could see the flicker of enemy campfires dotting the eastern slopes of South Mountain, only nine miles to the west.

Less than twenty-four hours later, on the eve of June 30, the first Northern soldiers appeared in Gettysburg in search of Lee's Army which was known to be in the vicinity. These men were General John Buford's division of cavalry which had been sent ahead to the area by General John F. Reynolds, commander of the First Corps and the advanced wing of the Union Army of the Potomac. After a long and dusty ride, the Federal cavalrymen entered Gettysburg from the south by way of the Emmitsburg Road where they were heartened by the sight of groups of loyal citizens who cheered and applauded as they approached. The horse soldiers, after placing pickets north and west of town, went into bivouac on the Edward McPherson, James J. Wills, and John Forney farms, just north and west of the Lutheran Theological Seminary.

Early on Wednesday, July 1, damp morning mist still lingering from the night before covered the advance units of Confederate General Henry Heth's Division, about 5,000 or 6,000 infantrymen, as they drew near the hushed village. At about eight o'clock in the morning they made contact with Buford's 3,000 horsemen posted west of the Seminary. The booming and crashing of the cannon and the scattering carbine and rifle fire marked the beginning of the three-day Battle of Gettysburg.

Soon after this initial conflict began, Rebel shells from the batteries west of the now fully awake community began to explode in and near the town. The commotion and serious danger resulting from these flying projectiles suggested to the populace that they should either hurry to their cellars for protection or leave their homes promptly for other refuges.

On that bloody morning, Jennie Wade decided that the house of her sister, Georgia, which was south of the town and near Cemetery Hill would be a much safer haven. It was there that she carried Isaac sometime before noon, leaving the boy with her mother. She then returned home to retrieve her youngest brother, Harry, and also to gather some essential clothing. As she inserted the key and turned the lock of her familiar and comfortable house on Breckenridge Street and dropped the key into the pocket of her dress, a melancholy Jennie may have had doubts of whether this war would permit her to ever return there again.

When she reached her sister's brick house which now sheltered her mother, sister and the newborn son, as well as the two boys, Jennie began to undertake the multitude of chores which had to be finished. She also answered the repeated knocks at the door by Union soldiers requesting food. A witness noted that, "After furnishing [them] bread, she brought water from the windlass well at the east side of the house to the dismounted cavalrymen stationed in front. She filled the canteens of these soldiers from a pail which she rested on the sidewalk."[27]

It was not long afterwards, only an hour or two, that hordes of defeated Yankee troops began their retreat from Seminary Ridge and Oak Ridge to the south side of town, an ebb which was caused by the breaking of the army's right flank in the afternoon. Standing along the dusty road and drenched from the waist down, Jennie offered cool, refreshing water to men who had been in the throes of battle, and were now hurrying southward from the distant ridges they had fought along all day. The sun was hot and oppressive and drinking water was in great demand. Jennie wore down a path to the well with her constantly empty pail as the "Boys in Blue" repeated their parched requests for water. [28]

Near five or six o'clock in the afternoon, new battle lines were being formed by both armies. The fighting of the first day had resulted in an incomplete Confederate victory. The Northern Army of the Potomac had been forced to retreat through the town into reserve positions on Culp's Hill and Cemetery Hill, both eminences, unfortunately, were within easy rifle range of the McClellan household.

The growing sense of insecurity felt by Gettysburg's inhabitants had been intensified as hundreds of these demoralized Federal soldiers were seen fleeing through the streets and alleys hotly pursued by the triumphant Rebels. Albertus McCreary remembered an officer who approached his house and warned, "All you good people go down to your cellars or you will be killed," at which McCreary said, "we obeyed him at once." Sarah Broadhead's diary that night recorded "bustle and confusion" and that "no one can imagine what extreme fright we were in when our men began to retreat." Union General Abner Doubleday, temporarily commanding the First Corps, later described how as his battered divisions passed through to the south, panic-stricken women begged the dispirited men not to abandon them to the Confederates.[29]

For those living in the lower sections of the town, peril of a different sort began to rear its ugly head. The Southerners seized various houses for sharpshooting purposes, seemingly unconcerned that the occupants might be caught in the deadly hail exchanged with Union riflemen on Cemetery Hill. John Will stated: "General Early warned the citizens...that we should go into our cellars and stay within our houses....He said that if at any moment the sharpshooters had spied us we might be picked off." Seventeen-year-old Anna Garlach remembered a Rebel soldier who burst into her family's Baltimore Street residence and climbed to the second floor. Anna's mother protested saying, "You can't go up there. You will draw fire on this house full of defenseless women and children." For this or for some other reason, the man departed.[30]

Henry Monath, a former member of Company I, 74th Pennsylvania Volunteers, wrote of his situation just outside of the McClellan house in an account published in 1897.

> ...our line lay back of the Battlefield hotel [Snyder's Wagon Hotel], about 100 yards. The ground was an orchard with large fruit trees. We were in close range with the sharpshooters from the houses in the city. [We]...received orders...to advance through the orchard of the hotel. The timothy was very high and on our hands and knees, we crawled forward to the hotel in great danger of being shot by the sharpshooters from the houses. Then [Lieutenant Joseph] Scheffer took half of the company into another house across the street; while in the house we were shooting at the rebels in other houses and they were firing at us....[31]

The Battlefield Hotel, circa 1884. Originally known as the Wagon Hotel, it was operated by Conrad and Catherine Snyder until 1860. To increase business, it was renamed Battlefield Hotel after the battle in 1863.

A Philadelphia newspaper created a similar scenario in this article:

> The houses in the immediate vicinity and an orchard on the side of the hill were occupied by Union sharpshooters, who had advanced from their line of battle on Cemetery Hill to engage a line of Confederate sharpshooters on the slight rise on the south of the town. The house of Mrs. McClellan was, however, never used as a protection for Union soldiers [sic].[32]

John Rupp, who lived in a frame house on Baltimore Street about 100 yards north of the McClellan home, was a tanner whose workshop was located at the rear of his house. He described his encounter with these keen-eyed marksmen in a letter a few days after the battle, to his sister, Anna, who lived in Baltimore.

> The rebs had my tannery in their possession for four days; they had the shop for a fort. It was full of rebs firing on our pickets up at [Solomon] Welty's fence....The rebs occupied the whole of town out as far as the back end of my house. Our men [occupied] that part of town which lays between our house and the cemetery, which is not much as you know, and the cemetery and all the high ground for miles around. Our men occupied my porch, and the rebel [men] the rear of the house, and I the cellar, so you can see that I was on neutral ground.

24

Our men knew I was in the cellar, but the rebs did not. I could hear the rebs load their guns and fire. There was one of our men killed under my big oak tree in the lot, and one in [Catherine] Snyder's meadow close to our house. The rebs occupied Mr. [Samuel] McCreary's house, from which they could pick off our men as they pleased. Our sharpshooters found it out and kept a look out, and finally shot one in Mr. McCreary's front upstairs and killed him on the spot, and also killed two up in Mr. [George] Schriver's house, next to Mr. [James] Pierce's. I sustained no loss in stock, but the rebs broke all the glass and sash in the shop. I gathered up a double handfull of Minie' balls in my dwelling after the battle, that were shot into it from both armies. If you could have heard the shells fly over our house from both sides! It was awful....It was awful thunder.[33]

Not far away, the Wades' abandoned Breckenridge Street house may have been taken over by Confederate soldiers operating in the vicinity, for the structures along that street offered a clear field of fire toward the Federal positions on Cemetery Hill and along the Emmitsburg Road.[34]

The McClellan house, the Wagon Hotel buildings, and the Dr. David Study and Captain John Myers houses, all on the northern slope of Cemetery Hill, were situated as if on a curved salient within the Union defensive line. Georgia's residence was dangerously only about fifty yards to the

The John Rupp Tannery, circa 1865. Smokestack is in left center distance with Battlefield Hotel at left and white dwelling on right adjacent to and blocking vision of McClellan house. Confederate sharpshooters occupied these structures in 1863.

25

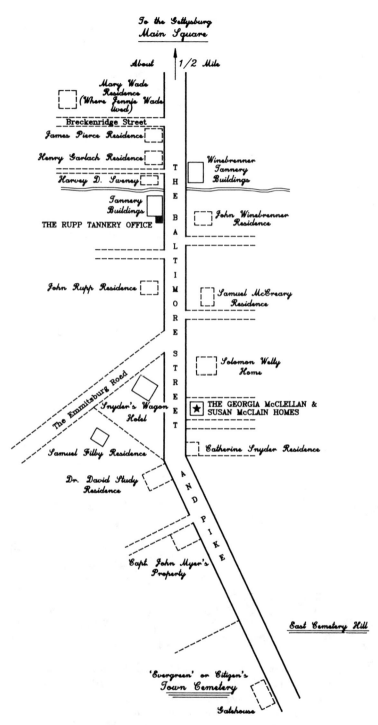

To the Gettysburg
Main Square

About 1/2 Mile

Mary Wade
Residence
(Where Jennie Wade
lived)

Breckenridge Street

James Pierce Residence

Henry Garlach Residence

Harvey D. Sweney

Tannery
Buildings
THE RUPP TANNERY OFFICE

Winebrenner
Tannery
Buildings

John Winebrenner
Residence

THE BALTIMORE STREET AND PIKE

John Rupp Residence

Samuel McCreary
Residence

Solomon Welty
Home

The Emmitsburg Road

Snyder's Wagon
Hotel

Samuel Filby Residence

Dr. David Study
Residence

★ THE GEORGIA McCLELLAN &
SUSAN McCLAIN HOMES

Catherine Snyder Residence

Capt. John Myer's
Property

East Cemetery Hill

'Evergreen' or Citizen's
Town Cemetery

Gatehouse

1863 map of some Baltimore Street residences. (Original by J. W.
Johnston, revised by Daniel E. Fuhrman)

east-southeast of this salient. Situated directly between the office of the Rupp Tannery buildings and the Union fortifications on East Cemetery Hill, the McClellan home posed as an advantageous location for Union sharpshooters. Most of these dwellings were likely secure hideouts for Yankee sharpshooters firing on their Southern counterparts who were slinking in and out of buildings on the south side of town in the John Winebrenner house, the John Rupp tannery site, and the Harvey D. Sweney home, among others.[35]

As evening approached it became obvious that the house which Jennie sought as a refuge was now quite the contrary. Rebel infantrymen stationed in the Rupp tannery on the opposite side of the street began firing at Union pickets around the small red brick structure which protected the women and children. The house was caught in a crossfire.

Due to this deadly hail of bullets, it was not long before a few Union soldiers fell seriously and mortally wounded within the McClellan yard and in a vacant lot to the north. One eyewitness recalled:

...Virginia Wade went out of the house on the evening of July 1st, and at the risk of her life brought water and cheer to those about who had fallen....William Otto Kahlar, of Co. 94, N.Y. Inf., writing from Lockport, N.Y...., report[ed] that Virginia Wade gave him two biscuits and a cup of water on July 1st, 1863. It seems that she also gave a cup to Orderly Sergeant Albert Brewer, who, it is said, has the souvenir to this day.[36]

Inside the house, the women were keeping themselves busy so they had little time to be frightened. The scene was described in this way:

Mrs. McClellan's bed had been taken down stairs in the spring of the year and placed in the parlor. The mother and her five days' old babe occupied the bed and the parlor room at the outbreak of hostilities. As night came on and the danger increased, the three women and three children found comfort in each other's company. Without disrobing the mother [Mary Wade] reclined on the bed with Mrs. McClellan and the child; while Virginia rested on a lounge under the window at the north side of the house. The two little boys did not mind trundle beds on the floor. Harry Wade having hidden under the bureau from time to time as the danger from the shots increased.[37]

The monotonous firing which reverberated around the sturdy walls of the McClellan house on the afternoon, evening and night of July 1, made rest almost impossible. The sweet oblivion of sleep became less and less attainable with each cry and groan that sounded from the wounded soldiers in the yard outside.

Chapter 5

"And over the hills the 'Blue and the Gray'
Were to meet and mingle their blood that day.
But the famished soldiers must be fed,
And Jennie's white hands must make them bread."

Shots from the Confederate outposts broke the stillness of dawn on the morning of Thursday, July 2. Union soldiers posted near the McClellan home returned the fire northward toward the tannery buildings and up death-swept Baltimore Street. During these dreadful days, the house was struck by fully 150 enemy bullets but, so far, it had not been the target of artillery, until that particular Thursday afternoon when the Wade family was faced with even more excitement. The splattering of rifle balls hitting the walls of the house was suddenly interrupted by the crash of a misdirected ten-pounder Parrott shrapnel shell likely fired from somewhere along Oak Ridge, two miles north of town. The screaming shell pierced a slanted roof over the stairway on the north side, passed through the wooden shingles and then penetrated into the plaster wall which divided the two houses of the double dwelling. The hurtling missile, continuing in its destructive path, plowed into the brick wall on the south side of the house, fortunately without exploding. The impact shook the twenty-one-year-old structure as if by an earthquake as it finally came to a halt above the exterior extension of the roof, where it would remain for over fifteen years.[38]

When she heard the crash of falling bricks, splintering wood and plaster raining down from the ceilings and walls upstairs, Jennie Wade, in that instant, fainted onto the floor.

Meanwhile the other occupants of the damaged house muttered silent prayers of gratitude that the treacherous projectile failed to explode. Had the shell's fuse functioned properly it could have killed or injured the Wades or Mrs. Catharine Freyburger McClain and her four children who lived in the southern portion of the double-dwelling. Ironically, thirty-four-year-old Catharine, who had just narrowly escaped death, was the widow of Isaac McClain, a Pennsylvania soldier who had been killed at Suffolk, Virginia, a short time prior to the Battle of Gettysburg.[39]

This erratic firing between the opposing lines was kept up during the eighty degree heat of the second day of the battle. Miraculously, there were no injuries to the inhabitants of the McClellan house, despite the risks taken by Jennie Wade as she carried water to the wounded Federals lying near the house and performed other brave acts of kindness, all the while dodging venomous bullets.

As the sultry day wore on, Jennie baked numerous batches of bread to feed the ravenous soldiers who were constantly banging at the door. Soldiers, it must have seemed to her, were always hungry. As her flour supply diminished, it became apparent that she had created an insurmountable demand for the home-baked bread the men had tasted and found so delicious. Consequently, Jennie and her mother were obliged to start more yeast which was mixed into sponge late on July 2 and left to rise until the next morning.

Frequent alarms and sporadic gunfire during that evening deprived the family of yet another night of uninterrupted rest. Tense and restless amidst the noise, the exhausted women lay partially awake wondering what new terrors the next day might bring. Jennie would have been even more restless had she known that only a mile or so away from where she slept, John Wesley Culp, present in the Rebel lines, possibly carried a message from Jack Skelly that was intended only for her. But Jennie did not know these things, and Wesley Culp was now encamped with his brigade only a short distance away from where his friend fitfully slept.

On that night of July 2 Wesley had obtained permission to enter Gettysburg to visit his sister, Barbara Ann Myers on West Middle Street. Just across the street lived Johnston and Elizabeth Skelly, the parents of his old schoolmate, Jack. This family was hiding at that moment in the commodious cellar of their neighbor, Harvey D. Wattles.[40]

Staying with Barbara Ann "Annie" Myers that evening was her younger sister, Julia, who later sought safety in the York Street cellar of her cousin, Mrs. William Stallsmith. Their parents, Esaias and Margaret Culp, were not alive during the Battle of Gettysburg. Wesley's, Annie's, and Julia's mother succumbed to "dropsy of the chest" in 1856 and their father, a tailor, died of paralysis in 1861. From what is known, it appears that Wesley Culp was very close to both of his sisters whom he visited on that July 2nd evening in Annie's home.[41]

A newspaper account would later detail Wesley's emotional visit.

That night there stepped jauntily into the Myers' home a sturdy, stocky figure, sunbronzed and weatherbeaten and clad in the rusty and somewhat tattered butternut, the uniform of the Army of Northern Virginia. There was a momentary pause as the stranger entered - and then a glad look of recognition as the sister cried, "Why Wes, you're here!" and then brother and sister were clasped in each other's arms as though there were no such things as war and horrors, and that deadly battle had been close at hand and would reopen with the day....Anna greeted him warmly, but warned that some relatives had threatened to "shoot the rebel on the spot" if they saw him. Wes smiled, ate his dinner....The talk fest began ....The hours passed. It grew late and finally Wes said he would have to go.

"Can't you stay until morning?" pleaded Mrs. Myers.

"No, Annie, I can't; but I'll come back in the morning, and I came near forgetting one important matter. Coming up through Winchester, I ran across Billy Holtzworth who was a prisoner in our hands. He told me about Jack Skelly being wounded and I hunted for poor Jack and had him taken to the hospital where we left him in charge of the Federal surgeons. He was badly shot through the arm. He gave me a message for his folks which I am to tell to his mother. It is late now and we will not disturb them, but you tell Mrs. Skelly I will be back in the morning and have her here. I want to talk to her and I'll be back sure."

"No message from Jack for anybody else in Gettysburg, Wes?" queried his sister. "Never mind," he replied, "you'll get all the news from Mrs. Skelly." His sisters promised to give her the message, but Wesley Culp said he had to deliver it in person.

"You ought to stay with us all night, Wes," called Mrs. Myers after him. "Come back. We may never see you again...."

But Wes was obdurate and made no response as he strode away in the darkness and returned to his company in line with the Stonewall Brigade [now commanded by General James A. Walker].[42]

Dough Trough. It was used to mix the flour and baking soda for biscuit dough and to store loaves of bread dough. Jennie was supposedly bent over this mixing tray kneading biscuit dough on the lid when she was shot.

Chapter 6

"...Oh, God! my feet are wet with blood!
What means this dark and clotted flood?
Alas! the tide is from her breast!
Her white hands there are tightly pressed... "

John Wesley Culp's sister, Annie, regrettably was only too correct in her premonition the night before of her sweet brother's fate, for,

> ...on July [3], [at around 8 o'clock in the morning] Wesley was killed on Culp's Hill [owned by his second cousin, Henry, and Peter Raffensberger]. Wesley's outfit, the famous "Stonewall Brigade" attempted to seize the hill from the Union forces. Wes was on the skirmish line when he was mortally wounded.[43]

Almost four hours earlier, Jennie Wade, completely unaware of the nearness of Culp or the possibility of a message from Jack Skelly that would fall silent with the death of her chum, Wesley, had already awakened to yet another day of bleak war. At four o'clock on Friday, July 3, 1863, the weary occupants of the McClellan house were still half asleep and no less apprehensive than they were the previous night. Jennie and young Harry cautiously slipped outdoors at about four thirty to fetch wood so that the fire could be revived in order to bake the bread dough which had been prepared the evening before.

When they returned to the still-warm kitchen, Jennie kneaded the dough and left it to rise again. Soon afterward a hungry Yankee soldier who had been driven back from one of the advance picket posts, came to the door asking for bread and was told to return later for a share of freshly made biscuits. Jennie was as generous as she could be when handing out these small kindnesses although there had been many opportunities to charge money for the food, as other Adams County inhabitants were doing. Even when the last soldier had called for nourishment at nine o'clock the night before, Jennie unselfishly saved only what was needed for the morning meal.[44]

After a frugal breakfast of bread, butter, applesauce and coffee, Jennie rested on the lounge in the parlor near the north window where she began her customary morning religious devotions. She read from Psalms XXVII to XXX commenting aloud, as a young person might normally do, on different passages. One verse in particular was her favorite:

> The Lord is my light and my salvation; whom shall I fear? The Lord is the strength of my life, of whom shall I be afraid?....Though war should rise against me, in this will I be confident...I had fainted unless I had believed to see the goodness of the Lord...Wait on the Lord; be of good courage, and he shall strengthen thine heart.

No one will ever know whether she opened her bible at this particular page by chance or intent, but the passages were singularly appropriate, for even now an invading host was encamped within a mile of where she sat, and war had indeed risen up against her, and she had need of all the "good courage" that was to be found in her own heart. Jennie most likely had no other wish than to be where she was at that moment. All the men she cared for - her eldest brother, her brother-in-law, and the man she loved, were all somewhere in the battle lines of the nation, and here was her opportunity to give something to the country's cause. But hearing such unpleasant words made her sister very uneasy about the undeniable danger they faced. Georgia begged her mother to command Jennie to stop and not intensify the already strained and uncomfortable situation. And, quite appropriately, the last words Georgia heard her sister utter were, "If there is anyone in this house that is to be killed today, I hope it is me, as George has that little baby."[45]

Near or about seven o'clock, the windows at the north side of their house unexplainably came under fire again by the Rebel marksmen. In mere seconds every pane of glass was shattered. One intruding bullet entered the front room and struck the bedpost, then hit the wall, and finally fell, an uninvited guest, onto the pillow at the foot of the bed where Georgia and her infant lay. The two had moved there earlier as a measure of safety, at Jennie's suggestion, because she believed that shots might come through the west door and window at any time. The bullet that burst through the north window was actually still warm when Mary Wade gathered it together, as a memento, with some wooden splinters from the damaged bedpost.[46]

The mantel clock had just chimed eight times when Jennie, determined to fulfill her commitment in spite of the musketry fire, started the preparations necessary to make the biscuits she had promised earlier. She slowly blended the flour and baking soda at her mixing tray as she had so many times the day before. The vigorous kneading of the dough was almost finished when Jennie asked her mother to start the stove fire for baking.[47]

It was a short half hour later, almost eight thirty, when a Confederate soldier, possibly one of the Louisiana infantrymen who had, throughout the last two days, been posted in buildings on both sides of Baltimore Street in southern Gettysburg, fired his weapon. No one will ever know his intended target. In fact it is possible he did not even have one, having been posted there to purposely harrass and intimidate Union soldiers along the north slope of Cemetery Hill. Indeed, the man may never have known or even cared where the one-ounce, soft-lead projectile came to rest. But in a split second, long before the large white puff of powder smoke dissipated from his weapon, Jennie Wade was dead. The hot lead had completed its deadly work, and the unknown assailant went about his dirty business, never realizing that a young woman, an innocent non-combatant, had just passed from mortal life. What should have been a solemn, tranquil or sad moment, was instead just another musket shot, hidden in its loud moment by the thunder of many others. To the killer, the life gone would have been simply another death undetected among so many, like the star that explodes with an inaudible bang in the silence of deep space.

The bullet itself had penetrated the outer door on the north side of the McClellan home and also the door which stood ajar between the parlor and the kitchen. It struck Jennie in the back just below the left shoulder blade. Her heart was pierced as the missile passed through and embedded itself in

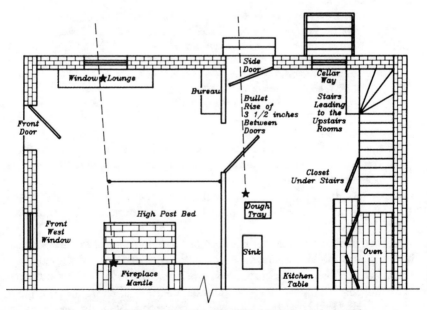

The Route of the Fatal Bullet. The dotted line through the side door shows the path taken by the deadly bullet. The line through the window marks the trail of the bullet that struck the bedpost shortly before Jennie's death. (Original by J. W. Johnston, revised by Daniel E. Fuhrman)

33

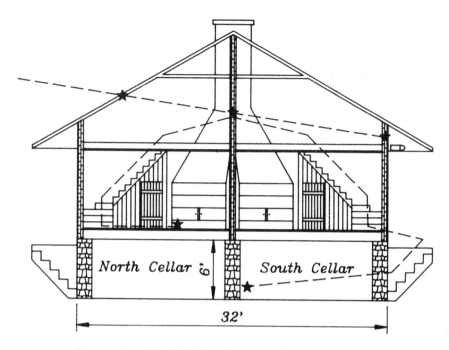

Cross-section of the McClellan House. The dotted line depicts the family's passage from the McClellan kitchen on the north side, through the hole in the wall upstairs and then into the McClain side to safety in the south cellar. The dotted line through the roof shows the route of the 10 pdr. Parrott shell on July 2. (Original by J.W. Johnston, revised by Daniel E. Fuhrman)

her corset at the front of her body. Her hands were still covered with the dough, which, along with the flour, was now scattered across the room.[48]

At the sounds of the bullet ripping its way through the wooden panels, Mrs. Wade turned from her work at the fire just in time to see her daughter fall. A hasty, terrifying examination made her realize what had happened. Almost calmly, she walked to the parlor and announced, "Georgia, your sister is dead." Overcome by the almost unthinkable news, Georgia screamed in alarm, a scream that brought several groups of Federal soldiers bursting into the kitchen from various places in and around the building. Upon hearing these cries of distress, one squad of New York infantrymen broke through the north door, which now clearly indicated the passage of the fatal missile. The dirty, battle-weary men stood solemnly looking at the body on the floor. Although dead bodies were no novelty to them, this one was different. Here was a woman, a Northern girl at that, who could easily have been a wife or sister of one of their own comrades.

After studying the situation, and a hurried discussion, they took charge

*Personal Property Found on the Body. This purse and photograph
of Jack Skelly were in Jennie's apron pockets when she was killed.*

35

at once. The men instructed the women to go quickly to their neighbor's cellar on the opposite side, the safer side, of the double-dwelling. How to get there, though, posed a problem. Normally, they would walk outside and around to the southern end of the house, then descend through the outside cellar doors. But now no one could exit through Georgia's dangerously exposed north wall as the Rebels were still showering bullets from that direction. However, it was observed that the shell which struck the house the day before had torn an opening in the wall upstairs that joined the dwellings. The soldiers quickly enlarged this ragged hole by tearing and kicking at the plaster and lath. Then the women were told to climb Georgia's stairs, pass through the opening and walk down the other stairway on the McClain side of the house where they could slip outside through the kitchen door to the cellar entrance a few feet away. In effect, the shell that came close to killing the Wade family the day before, now enabled them to protect their lives, in the end, by carving an interior route to safety that was undetectable by their adversaries.

Mary Wade agreed to obey as long as Jennie's body accompanied the family. So began their dangerous and morbid trek. With the baby in her arms and without assistance, Georgia ascended the stairs while a soldier followed carrying a split-bottom rocking chair. At the upstairs opening she handed the tiny bundle to another soldier as she crossed to the other side and then reclaimed her child. Mrs. Wade and the wide-eyed boys soon followed. Keeping their promise, the men, as tenderly as possible under the circumstances, carried Jennie's body through the same passage. Her body had been carefully wrapped in a quilt which Georgia had pieced together when she was only five years old.[49]

Once safely in the cellar, Jennie's corpse was placed on a wooden bench that was used to store milk pails and crocks. Still wrapped in the quilt, the pockets of Jennie's apron, unbeknownst to the people in the room at this time, held a photo of Corporal Skelly, a purse, and the key to the Wade home on Breckenridge Street. The lifeless body remained just inches away from the pathetic, dismal faces of her loved ones, there in the dim uncertain light of the cellar, from eight thirty on that morning of Friday, July 3, until one o'clock in the afternoon of the following day. For eighteen seemingly endless hours a vigil was reluctantly kept until finally the somber group felt safe enough to come out of their dreary hiding place.[50]

Urged on by the hungry soldiers, Mary Wade consented to return with them through the passageway to the desolate room upstairs stained with her child's blood. And with a heavy heart she forlornly baked fifteen loaves of bread using the dough which had been recently prepared by the daughter whom she loved so much. She must have reminded herself that Jennie would not have wanted the brave soldiers to go hungry. As she worked, Mrs. Wade kept her head turned away from the sinister dark stain on the cleanly scrubbed floor.[51]

Chapter 7

"...On the Fourth of July - our National day
They laid to rest her lifeless clay..."

Elsewhere in Gettysburg, civilians were contending with ordeals unlike any they had ever experienced. In the early afternoon of July 3, an artillery duel commenced involving approximately 230 cannon, which created a roar that seemed to Sarah Broadhead "as if heaven and earth were crashing together." For an hour and a half or longer it continued, appearing to the Broadhead family as though "the terrific sound of the strife" would never cease.[52]

Then as many of the guns fell silent, the Confederates massed approximately 12,000 men, many of them veterans of past battles, to hurl against the left center of the Army of the Potomac. This final and dramatic infantry assault which could have reversed the course of the war and decisively altered history, was soon in progress and its end quickly settled the conflict. By four o'clock that afternoon the Rebel attack had been repulsed, resulting in roughly 10,000 casualties for both sides. With the exception of some cavalry fighting on the flanks, armed combat at Gettysburg had come to an end.[53]

The town's civilian population, however, like the thousands in both armies, could not have known that the engagement was finally over. Throughout the evening hours all waited fearfully, while Sarah Broadhead wrote in her diary, "It would ease the horror if we knew our arms were successful."

During the evening hours rumbling sounds rising from Gettysburg's now desolate and filthy streets clearly indicated a vast movement of wagons, ambulances and artillery pieces. According to William H. Bayly, who lived on a farm three miles north of Gettysburg, wagon trains, stragglers, and camp followers began "drifting back in the direction whence they came." On the following morning, he found "that our host of visitors had, like the Arab, folded their tents and quietly stolen away."[54]

Very early on Saturday morning, the eighty-seventh birthday of the country, sometime near four o'clock, the Skelly family awakened to the martial music of the fife and drum. From their windows they saw a band "with the glorious Stars and Stripes fluttering at the head of the lines." Their reaction was, "Ye gods! What a welcome sight for the imprisoned people of Gettysburg." As the morning progressed and the Rebel evacuation clearly was underway the citizens were, in the words of Robert F. McClean, "a happier set of people you never saw." [55]

Yet the dread and tension did not disappear entirely. Matilda "Tillie" Pierce, a fifteen-year-old that memorable year, said, "We were glad that the storm had passed and that victory was perched on our banners but, oh, the horror and desolation that remained." [56] For most of the population the worst was yet to come - many grim weeks of struggling to cope with the aftermath of war - with over twenty thousand wounded soldiers in and around the village, and the thousands of decomposing corpses of men and horses and mules which had been slaughtered.

An aura of melancholia surrounded the little brick house on Baltimore Street. The grief-stricken Wade family was preoccupied with their own single casualty - Mary Virginia Wade. And on July 4, Georgia's twenty-second birthday, it had rained early in the morning and then again from 2:15 in the afternoon until about four o'clock, which added to the overall misery of the situation. An hour after the rain stopped, a small gathering consisting of Jennie's mother, her sister, her grandmother Mrs. Elizabeth Filby, her brother Harry and about six or eight soldiers stood in the humid seventy degree weather near a muddy, gaping grave which had been prepared in the now trampled garden at the rear of the house. A curious incident accompanied the burial:

> Jennie's body had been carried from the cellar and placed in a coffin on the brick pavement outside the cellar doors on the south side of the house. It is believed that Jennie's casket was originally intended for a Confederate officer with the initial construction done by Confederate soldiers. This coffin was completed by Mr. Charles Comfort of Gettysburg.[57]

Since preparations were not made for the cleansing, embalming or redressing of Jennie's body, it was merely placed in the coffin with the quilt snuggly wrapped about it. "The dough...was still on her hands and arms as Jennie was lowered into the ground in the yard of her sister's home." [58] "...There were no prayers, no hymns. Jennie's mother, her sister, and her two little brothers stood silently with bowed heads as the clods fell on the pine box." [59]

Jennie's body would remain in this primitive grave from the afternoon of July 4 until January of the following year when it was removed to the cemetery adjoining the nearby German Reformed Church. A story kept alive by the family for many generations was that, "when Jennie's remains were moved from the back yard..., the body had mummified" or in the vernacular of the day, "she had turned to stone."[60]

In November of 1865, fully two years to the month since Abraham Lincoln had stood in the same cemetery to deliver a eulogy over the graves of thousands of fallen warriors, Georgia's husband, Louis, and her brother, John, transferred Jennie's body to the family plot John had bought in the Evergreen Cemetery where it still lies today.[61]

Even after the pathetic burial of her daughter, additional trouble followed Mary Wade as she returned to her house on Breckenridge Street. On the evening of July 5, just twenty-four hours since she stood by the grave of her child, Mrs. Wade entertained a visitor, Reverend [Walter S.] Alexander, a delegate of the U.S. Christian Commission, who quite likely had come to comfort the woman during her time of grief. Also in the house was Major Michael William Burns, 73rd New York Infantry, who had commanded his regiment during the late battle. It is still a mystery as to why Burns was in the Wade dwelling and not with his regiment. But there is no doubt some sort of altercation took place as a grossly intoxicated Burns assaulted the minister and inflicted a serious sword wound to his head. Burns was promptly arrested, but the brutal scene must have finally broken the spirit of Mary Wade.[62]

Jennie Wade's Birthplace. An historical plaque, unveiled in 1922, marks the building at the crest of Baltimore Street hill.

Chapter 8

"...Fell at her task, as the soldier dies
Cold in her beauty our heroine lies..."

The long, hot summer days following the battle were chaotic, unnerving and turbulent among many inhabitants of the community. In a strange reversal of the truth, the first newspaper story about the shooting actually described Jennie's killer as a Union marksman. The following interesting account appeared on July 7, 1863 in the Adams *Sentinel:*

> But withal, we have been called to part with some. We have learned only of the following: - Killed, Miss Virginia Wade by our own sharpshooters.... The suffering and afflicted need not be assured that they have the hearty sympathy of the entire community.

Quickly, the news of the only civilian killed among them was carried by soldiers, newspaper reporters, neighbors, friends and even some townspeople who pretended to know Jennie. Throughout the days, weeks, months and years to follow, some enlisted men and officers would recall Jennie's death in their journals and regimental records. For instance, Captain Emil Koenig of the 58th New York Infantry, 11th Army Corps, submitted this story in his report of the three-day battle:

> ....At 6 o'clock in the morning, [July 3] we were ordered to the right of the road leading to Gettysburg. We were posted behind a stone fence to the left of Captain [Michael] Wiedrich's [New York] battery. Lieutenant [Carl] Schwartz, with one company, was sent to take possession of the next houses of the town to the left of the road. The enemy's sharpshooters kept up a brisk fire at these houses, and killed a girl who was living in one of them. Our men escaped uninjured, although they had possession of the house until the end of the battle, and the house was completely pierced by bomb-shells and rifle-balls.

John Y. Foster, a civilian from Philadelphia, arrived in Gettysburg on the evening of July 10 and worked with the U.S. Christian Commission at the

Second Corps field hospital three miles south of Gettysburg. He recounted this story:

> ...a woman named Wade was engaged in baking bread for our troops in a house situated directly in range of the guns of both armies. The rebels had repeatedly ordered her to quit the premises, but she had invariably refused to do so. At length the battle opened, and while still engaged in her patriotic work a ball pierced her loyal breast, and she fell. Was not that genuine heroism?....[63]

Robert S. Robertson, a 93rd New York Infantryman, wrote in the July 6 entry of his diary:

> ...some of the women who staid home proved to be heroines and did all in their power to aid the wounded....One young girl, I heard, was killed while making bread for the soldiers, the house she was in having been in musket range of the rebels.[64]

Abram P. Smith, 76th New York Volunteers, noted in a regimental history that:

> ....The people of Gettysburg...are heartily loyal. At many of the doors and windows, the ladies, lads and girls stood through that long, hot day, and passed water and food to the Union troops. The men of the Seventy-sixth will not soon forget, and I should fail in the performance of my duty, did I not mention the "nameless heroine," who, with a cup in each hand, so busily dealt out water to the thirsty boys, the tears of sympathy streaming down her lovely cheeks, as the wounded soldiers came hobbling by, until, pierced by a rebel ball, she fell dead by the side of her pail! We regret that we cannot hand down her name to posterity, even in these humble pages. The memory of her deeds and heroic sacrifice shall remain green, though her name is unknown.[65]

Civilian Susan T. McClain was a two-year-old baby who lived with her mother and three siblings in the other half of the McClellan house that July of 1863. She recalled being told that the killing of Jennie Wade occurred this way:

> My mother and my three brothers and sisters were living in the basement at the time because a shell had gone through the house only a few days before. Miss Wade was baking bread in the kitchen upstairs.
> She had just stepped to the door with an armful of dough to ask her sister if she thought that would make enough bread when the bullet struck her. She

died very quickly.

[My] mother told [me] the slain woman was taken to the basement, where she lay for two full days before some of her fellow townsmen buried her in the garden.

I'm not sure about it though....I was too young to know much about what was going on. [66]

Another account of a civilian learning the news of Jennie's death was that of Elizabeth Thorn. Her husband, Peter, was away in the army near Harper's Ferry, Virginia at the time of the Gettysburg battle and Mrs. Thorn, with her family, lived in the Gateway House while they tended to the maintenance of the Evergreen Cemetery. When the hostilities forced them to move southward out of town for safety, Mrs. Thorn approached the Henry Beitler house looking for something to eat for her bedraggled companions. After a knock on the door...

An officer came out and asked us what we wanted. He had been in town and said to us, "Did you know Jennie Wade?" I said I knew her, that she lived near my home. He then told us she got killed. He asked whether we knew Maria Bennet, that she [too] got killed but this turned out to be a false report.... [67]

John Rupp, quoted earlier, who had spent several days in his cellar just yards from the McClellan house, mentioned news of Jennie's death in a letter dated July 19, to his sister, Anne, who lived in Baltimore. The sharpshooter whose fatal bullet hit Jennie was allegedly in, and has commonly been noted to have been at, Rupp's tannery office when he fired the now well-known shot.

....Virginia Wade was killed while kneading up her bread, for her sister, up in the house that Ellen Freeberger used to live. Several others were hit on the shins with spent balls, where, if they had stayed in their houses, would not have happened [to] them. I can't tell you all; it would take me a week to do so. Our house is pretty well riddled; though balls passing through our bedsteads, no shells struck it. [68]

A neighbor of Georgia McClellan, four-year-old Rosa A. Snyder, lived with her mother Catherine, and her five brothers and sisters on the east side of Baltimore Street, just before it turned into the Baltimore Turnpike. Nearly eighty years later, Miss Snyder remembered:

....The next-door neighbors, the Wade family, had gone to their cellar too, but not in time to save the life of 16-year-old [sic] Jennie Wade. Jennie was in the kitchen kneading dough for "shortcake." A bullet entered the outside door of the Wade home, penetrated the bedroom door which was opened into the hallway and struck Jennie in the back. Jennie, the only civilian killed in Gettysburg, fell within a few feet of her mother, some pieces of dough still in her fingers....[69]

Another woman, Sophronia E. Bucklin who worked as a volunteer nurse after the battle, noted, "....Sometimes we went, in our rambles [for food and supplies], to various stores; [and] out into the surrounding country. In one of these I saw the hole in the door made by the bullet which struck the maiden, Jennie Wade, to the heart, as she stood moulding her bread at the table...."[70]

At the age of seventy-seven in 1928, Mary Warren Fastnacht wrote her memories of the battle, which occurred when she was twelve years old. She recalled the trip from her father's house on West Middle Street to her grandfather's house on Baltimore Street: "I will never forget that walk in the early morning. Men and horses were lying in the street. Up at Grandfather's home we all had to go to the cellar. While there word came that Jennie Wade had been shot, just two blocks away. She was buried in their garden until later removed to Evergreen Cemetery...."[71]

Hugh M. Ziegler dictated his reminiscences in April and May of 1933. He, it seems, watched the confusion of the battle through the eyes of a ten-year-old. "Few of the citizens were injured and but one was killed. Jennie Wade who was in her kitchen baking bread for the soldiers was killed by a stray bullet that came in at one of the windows."[72]

As time went by, people began to embroil the simple saga as they knew it or thought it should be, into a mudslinging contest to achieve personal gain, and to trumpet their own acts of patriotism whether true or false. Through the use of personal attacks these publicity mongers criticized each other while hiding behind their political parties, their community as a whole, or through individuals like John Burns. Some outright falsehoods resulted from these attacks, the nature of which belittled the deeds of some to exaggerate those of others. Many would say it was a good thing Jennie was not alive to hear some of the slurs that were thrown her way. For instance, there was a heated exchange of journalistic fire between the Harrisburg *Telegraph* and the Adams *Sentinel and General Advertiser* of Gettysburg. The Harrisburg paper claimed,

Old [John] Burns was the only man of Gettysburg who participated in the struggle to save the North from invasion, while innocent Jenny [sic] Wade was the only sacrifice which the people of that locality had to offer on the shrine of their country....Let a monument be erected on the ground which covers her,...If the people of Gettysburg are not able alone to raise the funds to pay for a suitable monument for Jenny Wade, let them send a committee to Harrisburg, and our little boys and girls will assist in soliciting subscriptions for this holy purpose....

In an obviously defensive rebuttal, the *Sentinel* of December 1, 1863 stated:

The friends of Miss Wade have the deep sympathy of our people, while Mr. Burns' patriotism receives its full mead of praise, and no community has given evidence of its willingness to render both promptly and fully - ribald newspaper correspondents to the contrary notwithstanding. We do not know that it is necessary for our people to go abroad to seek inspirations of patriotism of duty. At all events, we feel assured, they would hardly go to Harrisburg for lessons in this respect, if one fourth of what has been written and printed of the doings of the goodly citizens of that place during the memorable days of June and July, be true....

While doing justice to the patriotic impulses of John Burns - an old man of 70 years - it is not necessary to utter the falsehood that he "was the only man of Gettysburg who participated in the struggle to save the north from invasion." Gettysburg has sent to the field, since the beginning of the War, more than one half of its voting population. The blood of her sons has freely mingled with that of the heroes of the Republic on more than one hard- fought field. Can the *Telegraph* say as much for Harrisburg?

The death of Miss Wade is made the occasion of another equally malicious assault on the reputation of our people, in the statement that this "was the only sacrifice which the people of that locality had to offer on the shrine of their country." - Possibly it might have suited the fancy of the *Telegraph* editor to have recorded the slaughter of more of our innocent women and children by rebel bullets. Fortunately we can boast of but one. But if Mr. Bergner means to affirm that the ladies of this community - town and county - made few or light sacrifices during the terrible scenes of July last, he simply lies - as thousands of suffering, wounded soldiers, and hundreds of christian men and women, summoned here on errands of love and mercy, can well attest....

And in that same issue of the paper, a short article directly followed the abovementioned, written from the *Lutheran Missionary* in Philadelphia, which read:

The hospitable people of Gettysburg kept open house during the crowded days....Immense was the mass of people thrown upon that community, of some two or three thousand souls, we have not yet heard a person speak in any other than the warmest terms of the comfort he enjoyed and the welcome he received. The people of Gettysburg need not fear comparison with those of any town or city in our State. Their conduct before the great battles, and during them, and since then, has been in the highest degree honorable. The miserable libels which were invented to their injury, have simply directed attention more closely to their real excellence.

And so it went. Gettysburg and Adams County would continue to proclaim, defend, and even justify the conduct of its citizens for years to come.

Mary Wade Residence. Abandoned by the Wade family during the battle, this was the home of Jennie Wade at that time.

Chapter 9

"...And what of her lover fond and true?
He followed her soon in his suit of blue;
At 'Carter's Woods' he was wounded and fell..."

John Wesley Culp was not the last of Jack Skelly's visitors in that hospital situated on Virginia's enemy soil. John Warner, the 87th Pennsylvania Infantry's sutler, visited Jack on Saturday, July 11 at Taylor House Hospital. Warner described Skelly as badly wounded and delirious at the time of his visit. Jack did not recognize Warner who was told by the surgeon that he did not have long to live. Warner remembered:

> When I saw him he did not seem to be suffering, just lying in a stupor. The boys in the company and I knew he corresponded regularly with Jennie Wade, but we did not know of their engagement and intended marriage.
> ....Wes Culp had carried the tidings of Jack being wounded. If he had any other messages of course I had no chance to know of them. Wes saw Jack when he was able to talk and knew his condition.[73]

Johnston Hastings Skelly, Jr. died the next day, July 12, just nine days after Jennie's and Wesley's untimely deaths. How tragic, or perhaps merciful, that these three young friends were completely unaware of each other's fate. The note or verbal message given to Wesley Culp by Jack Skelly was never delivered. Since they all died just a few days apart, and Wesley refused to divulge the contents to anyone but the intended recipient, there was no way to ever determine just what Skelly wanted his mother to know, or, as some believe, what message poor Jack Skelly wanted his mother to pass on to Jennie Wade.

Skelly was initially buried in the Lutheran Cemetery in Winchester, Virginia, but by November of 1864, Jack's brother, Daniel, returned his body to Gettysburg where it was interred in the Evergreen Cemetery, only a few hundred feet from Jennie's beautiful gravesite. On April 15, 1880, the trustees of the Methodist Episcopal Church on East Middle Street sold their old meetinghouse to the local chapter of the Grand Army of the Republic (G.A.R.), a Civil War veterans organization. The "Corporal Skelly Post

No.9, G.A.R.," retained the building for fifty-three years and honored the memory of Johnston Hastings Skelly, Jr. by bearing his name.[74]

Corporal Skelly's Grave. His second interment was on November 30, 1864.

Chapter 10

"...By the soldier's lonely bed,
In the midnight dark and dread,
'Mid the wounded and the dead,
with lifeblood pouring red... "[75]

The last few days of that bitter July, 1863, and just three weeks after the death of her sister, Georgia left her baby with her mother to serve as a nurse to the sick and wounded soldiers in the Adams County Court House at Gettysburg, which was being used as a hospital. She remained there for one week when she was transferred to the United States Army General Hospital at Wolf's Grove, known as Camp Letterman, two miles east of Gettysburg. Georgia worked hard intermittently for the next two years tending to wounded and ill soldiers on several other battlefields, offering her compassionate assistance wherever she could, while her husband was away serving in the Army.[76]

Her mother, at home in Gettysburg with the baby, Louis Kenneth, keeping her busy, was surprised and honored to receive a letter from President Lincoln shortly after the battle expressing his praise and condolence in the death of Jennie while so diligently serving the soldiers of her country. And when Lincoln visited Gettysburg on November 18-19, 1863 to dedicate the Soldiers' National Cemetery, he requested that Georgia McClellan sit with him on the speakers' platform among the other dignitaries. She did not want to go, but her mother insisted since the President invited her. Later, Georgia said that she would have left prior to President Lincoln's address if she could have found a way to slip off the platform while the principal orator Edward Everett recited his long but eloquent speech.[77]

In 1867 Georgia and her husband, Louis, moved to Denison, Iowa to join their friends, the H.C. Laub family who had gone west from Pennsylvania a few years earlier. During those early days on the plains Georgia was the only nurse in Denison and frequently was pressed into the medical service she had come to know so well. Georgia and Louis had five children: Louis Kenneth (the baby born just before the battle), Virginia Wade, James Britton, Nellie G. and John Harry. Engaging in Women's Relief Corps work

Georgia Wade McClellan, in front of the McClellan house in 1913, when she traveled to Gettysburg for the 50th Anniversary of the Battle of Gettysburg.

after the war, an auxiliary to the Grand Army of the Republic, Georgia held many offices in this organization at the national, state and local levels. In 1898 the 10th New York Cavalry made Georgia an honorary member of their veterans organization. This unit had been quartered in Gettysburg during the winter of 1861-62 and had come to know the Wade family through the kindnesses they displayed to the soldiers.[78]

Georgia Wade McClellan died in Carroll, Iowa on September 7, 1927, at the age of eighty-six. She never received her nurse's pension in person, as it arrived the day after she died, but she had received a widow's pension following the death of her husband in 1913.[79]

Like Georgia, all of her brothers also moved west and lived out the rest of their lives there. John James Wade who last saw his sister Jennie as she devotedly altered his uniform on June 26, 1863, had, himself, moved to Denison, Iowa in 1866. From there he traveled west with the Union Pacific Railroad to California. He later resided in Nevada for a while until he moved again and married a Texan, Julia F. Rush, on March 17, 1875 in Clover Valley, Colorado. They made their home in Mancos, Colorado for forty-two years where John and Julia had five children who he supported through various trades as farmer, carpenter and a miner over the years. He died in Kayenta, Arizona in Navajo County on September 2, 1925.[80]

As he grew older, brother Samuel, who as a twelve-year-old was arrested

49

then released for trying to save his employer's horse from the enemy's grasp, lived in Gettysburg with his wife, Elizabeth Johns or "Lizzie" from York Springs, Pennsylvania, whom he married on November 17, 1869, a time when he worked as a housepainter. Later, they moved to Peoria, Illinois, where he died some time around 1927.[81]

Harry, the eight-year-old brother who witnessed his sister's death in the McClellan house kitchen, first moved to Nebraska and then to Seattle, Washington, where he married his wife, Mary. He died there at the age of fifty-five, on September 26, 1906.[82]

Very little is still known about James Wade, Sr., Jennie's father, who died on July 10, 1872 at the age of fifty-eight years, eleven months. He spent his last years a sick, broken man, in the Adams County Alms House, listed in the register as a "pauper." James Wade was buried on July 11 in the Evergreen Cemetery, Lot 79, Section A.[83]

If there was anyone who felt the true depth of tragedy in the loss of Jennie, it was Mary Wade. Not only did she lose a loving, selfless daughter, but she felt the void of Jennie's financial support in a time when every penny went to maintaining the family's stability. Twenty years after Jennie's death her mother was granted monetary aid from the government as retribution. In July of 1871, Mary Wade collected the then large sum of $1,440 as compensation of $8.00 per month since the day Jennie was killed. The pension report testified that Jennie was, "a healthy girl, very faithful, steady

Mary Ann Filby Wade. Mother of Mary Virginia Wade, 1820-1892. This photograph was taken two years before her death.

and expert with the needle, who at the time of her death and for some years previous thereto, contributed materially to the support of the family." Johnston H. Skelly, Sr. and William T. King, merchant tailors, made oath in the report that both Mary and Jennie Wade had worked for them at the tailoring trade.[84]

Mary may have found some comfort in the company of her parents, Samuel and Elizabeth, who resided in a house near where Jennie had been killed. Despite the war and other hardships, She continued to sew and do laundry which enabled her to keep her house on Breckenridge Street until she died in 1892, when she was seventy-two years old. Mary Ann Filby Wade was buried in the Evergreen Cemetery on December 31, 1892. In her last will and testament, Mary Wade's property was divided equally among her children and in January, 1893, as power-of-attorney, her daughter, Georgia, sold the property to Adam Ertter who utilized it as an income property.[85]

And, finally, what became of the newborn baby whose entrance into the world caused Jennie and her family to gather at the deadly McClellan house? Louis Kenneth McClellan became known by historians, and the public alike, as the "youngest veteran of the Battle of Gettysburg." In his adult years, he moved to Montana in 1906 where he resided in Billings for sixteen years. Among other things, he was an inventor of sorts and was married with two sons. He died after a two-year illness in Billings on February 12, 1941, Lincoln's birthday, at the age of seventy-seven.[86]

Louis Kenneth McClellan. He was born just five days before the battle, and later lived in Billings, Montana.

Chapter 11

*"A maiden fair as the flag that waves
Over her tomb 'mid the soldiers' graves..."*

Until the year 1900, in the brand new century, Jennie Wade's grave had been unmarked save by a small tombstone. Each year on Memorial Day her resting place was decorated with flowers and a tiny American flag added by her friends and members of the Grand Army of the Republic Post of Gettysburg. Then in June of that same year, the Iowa Woman's Relief Corps (W.R.C.), of which Georgia McClellan was National Executive Board Chairman, voted at their department convention to erect a monument to the memory of Mary Virginia Wade. There were no regiments from the state of Iowa in the battle, hence, no Iowa state monuments. A January, 1901 Iowa newspaper said: "Because of the noble deeds of Jennie Wade and her relationship to a noted Iowa lady it is most fitting that the Iowa W.R.C. erect the memorial in contemplation....of the only woman who lost her life, directly in the line of patriotic duty in this, the most memorable battle of the civil war." [87]

Funds to erect the monument were solicited by the Iowa Woman's Relief Corps and were received from the Iowa Corps, from Missouri, and from friends and members of the Wade family scattered throughout this country and even from other nations. The cost of the monument, which was designed in Italy, was $1,200, the bulk of which the Gettysburg Battlefield Commission paid $1,000 on behalf of the subscribers. Mrs. Anna Miller, the designer, contractor and former operator of a marble cutting business, donated $200. [88]

Although it was erected on August 17, 1900, the Jennie Wade monument was not unveiled until more than a year later on September 16, 1901 during a beautiful ceremony which included music, invocations and speeches given by Georgia McClellan and other officers of the W.R.C. The inscription on the monument was read aloud, "Jennie Wade, killed July 3, 1863, while making bread for Union soldiers." On the opposite side appears, "Erected by the Woman's Relief Corps of Iowa, A.D. 1901." The Wade family motto, "Whatsoever God Willeth Must be, Though a Nation Mourns," is on the third side, and on the remaining face the simple epitaph, "She Hath Done

Seated left to right: Anna Garlach Kitzmiller, Georgia Wade McClellan, Robert C. Miller. Standing left to right: Mrs. Ida Kitzmiller Mumper, Mrs. Anna Louise Kitzmiller Miller, Harold Mumper, Georgia Wade Schwarzenbach, Anna Miller (later became Weaver), Charles Kitzmiller Miller (Anna's twin brother). (Photo by Jacob Ira Mumper, circa 1910. Courtesy of Patricia Weaver Newton.)

What She Could." [89]

Nine years later, with Georgia McClellan in attendance from Iowa, a steel flagstaff was placed near Jennie's grave by the Gettysburg Association of Iowa Women on which the American flag is flown night and day. In 1917, it was noted that a new flag was sent each year by Iowa's Woman's Relief Corps. [90]

In addition to the statue of Jennie Wade, the McClellan house where she was killed also serves as a shrine to her patriotic sacrifice. About the turn of the century, the first combined museum and souvenir business was set up by Robert C. Miller at this house. The hole in the door that was a clear reminder of the path traveled by the fatal bullet, was a strong drawing card. In 1956, a Gettysburg newspaper claimed that,

A few original pieces of furniture that are still in the museum today are the large clock and four-legged wooden stool which were in the McClain half (south) of the house at the time of the Battle....The clock has been placed on the mantel in the room used by the McClains as their kitchen where it no doubt stood during the battle. [91]

The Mary Virginia Wade Monument. Erected in 1900 in Evergreen Cemetery, it is only 100 paces from the grave of Johnston Hastings Skelly, Jr.

"Jennie Wade House" Museum. First combined museum and souvenir business opened in Gettysburg in early 1900.

The North Door. The hole made by the fatal bullet is near the doorknob where the circle is drawn. Bricks around the door are pitted with the marks of Confederate bullets.

The following are a few of several notes left concerning the museum that were prepared by William G. Weaver, who gathered the information for the owner:

The doughtray in the front room is absolutely the original. It has on it a photostatic copy of the affidavit that accompanied it and signed by Mrs. McClellan,...The bullet hole in an upper pane of glass in the north window of the front room is original. There is another hole in the upper frame of the lower sash of the same window. When the lower sash is raised, as it was during the battle, the two holes match exactly. They were made by the same bullet; it spent itself against the chimney across the room....I was often asked why the door was not replaced or repaired since it has three holes in it. I asked Mrs. [Robert C.] Miller that question. She said that her father, who was a Civil War veteran, was very proud of the historical significance of the house and he was glad to live in a house that bore the many bullet marks that it did.[92]

Another recognition of the memory of Jennie Wade came about in the year 1864 in the form of songs. At least two versions of a song honoring her made their appearance - one published in Philadelphia, the other in Cleveland. While the pieces had different tunes, their words were almost identical although credited to different authors.[93]

A final tribute to Jennie was the placement of a historical tablet on the house at the crest of Baltimore Street where she was born. The inscription on the plaque reads "Mary Virginia Wade. A heroine of the Battle of Gettysburg, was born in this house, May 21, 1843. This tablet was unveiled by her sister, Georgia Wade McClellan, May 21, 1922." Today, her house on Breckenridge Street is mostly unnoticed by the average visitor to Gettysburg.[94]

Chapter 12

"...Ne'er from this country's altars fade
The memory of Jennie Wade!"

The certain fact remains that *The Jennie Wade Story* you have just completed is and always will be an intricate part of the historiography of what is no doubt one of the most important single events in American history. The Gettysburg Campaign and battle came and went like a thunderbolt, and in many ways the world for thousands, even millions of people, was never the same again. The battle has been called the "High Water Mark of the Rebellion" or even the "turning point" of the great Civil War - and Mary Virginia Wade is part and parcel of that grand and terrible time. For three days the world waited while titans clashed, and mighty armies brought steel and iron and lead, and human flesh together in a landscape of death and destruction never before equaled in the Western Hemisphere. Jennie Wade was there. She was a spectator and a participant both, in this fantastic drama. Her story deserves to be repeated as it has always been told, for it shall forever remain among the most alluring lore of Gettysburg.

The End

"...Soldiers write the songs
that soldiers sing
the songs that
you and I won't sing
let's not look the other way
taking a chance
because if the bugler
starts to play
*we **too** must dance....."*

ABBA
1981

APPENDIX I

Other Civilian Losses During and After the Battle of Gettysburg

Mary Virginia Wade was the only Gettysburg civilian killed during the battle, but she was not the only citizen who was hit while the fighting raged with bullets, shells and canister flying in all directions.

Three men were wounded in town by stray shots or by Confederates who assumed they were either Federals or were up to no good. Jacob Gilbert, a Gettysburg resident for many years, was struck in the upper left arm while walking on Middle Street. A "Mr." Lehman of Pennsylvania College was wounded in the leg. R.F. McIlhenny was injured in his ankle. And Amos Moser Whetstone, a Seminary student who boarded with "old Mrs. [Nancy] Weikert" on Chambersburg Street, was shot in the thigh by a sharpshooter on July 4.

Two civilians who were wounded as they voluntarily joined military units were John Burns and J.W. (or C.F.) Weakley. By the end of the first day of fighting, 71-year-old John Burns had been wounded three times: in his upper thigh, in the leg and in his left arm. None of the wounds proved to be serious. Weakley was a boy from Maryland who had followed the First Corps from Emmitsburg, Maryland, begging all the while to be allowed to enlist in the army. About fifteen years old at the time, he was taken in by the veterans of Company A of the 12th Massachusetts Infantry who gave him a makeshift uniform and weapon. Weakley was wounded in the arm and thigh as he fought with the regiment, although he had not yet been mustered into service. Months later, he officially was enrolled in a U.S. Maryland regiment and was discharged for disability in 1864.

On July 1, an incident occurred involving the fatal shooting of a chaplain, a non-combatant with the 90th Pennsylvania Infantry. Chaplain Horatio S. Howell was standing on the steps of the Christ Lutheran Church on Chambersburg Street when he was shot and instantly killed by a Rebel soldier.

On July 3 at about one o'clock, a shell from one of the signal guns preceding Pickett's Charge exploded in William Patterson's barn on the Taneytown Road. The shell tore off the arm of a fourteen-year- old black boy who was the servant of a New York soldier. And James Godman, a black man in the Southern army at Gettysburg, was killed in action during the battle.

The following are a few of the civilian casualties which occurred after the battle, hence, they were not a direct result of the fighting.

The July 7, 1863 edition of the Adams *Sentinel* claimed that "...Edward M., son of Alexander Woods, [was] shot accidentally by his brother, while playing with a gun picked off the battlefield."

Albertus McCreary recalled in *McClure's* in 1909, "A schoolmate of mine found a shell, he struck it upon a rock and made a spark which exploded the shell. We carried him to his home, and the surgeons did what they could, but he died in about an hour." McCreary also remembered, "The only other accident that I witnessed happened a year after the Battle. I was passing along High Street, and had reached Power's stoneyard, when I heard a terrible explosion behind me. I saw a young schoolmate lying on his back with his bowels blown away. Near him was a man almost torn to pieces, his hands hanging in shreds."

In 1929, Charles M. McCurdy's memoirs recalled that two of his chums were killed several months after the battle while trying to open unexploded artillery shells.

Another episode was registered in September of 1863 when Michael Crilly was engaged in an effort to unload a shell, it exploded and seriously injured his hand, requiring the amputation of three fingers. And in March of 1864, several fifteen-year-old boys were amusing themselves with a gun from the battlefield, when the contents discharged and entered the head of a little seven-year-old black girl, inflicting a mortal wound. In June of that year, Adam Taney, Jr., residing in Fairfield, had a serious accident while attempting to open a shell found in a field. The shell exploded and some of the fragments struck him in the feet, which possibly crippled him for life.

A section of floorboard from the McClellan house stained with the blood of Jennie Wade. It was saved as a valuable relic of the battle by Ida May Kitzmiller when the original floor was replaced. (Courtesy of Patricia Weaver Newton and Jamie L. Newton of Gettysburg, PA.)

APPENDIX II

The Moral Factor in Determining the Reputation of Mary Virginia Wade

Justified or not, Mary Virginia Wade's reputation has been questioned by many people who have heard the story of her death at Gettysburg. A common thread that weaves throughout is the rumor that she may have been a woman of loose virtue or morals. Most people hear or read a short narrative of Jennie's death and know essentially nothing more than a paragraph's worth about her life. Hence there is much speculation based on no sources of substance or real evidence other than the fact that a basically innocent small- town girl was doing the best she could during a very difficult time. No particular interest would have been taken in Jennie if her life had not been snuffed out during such a singularly important and significant event in our country's history.

The only possible identification of this theme was the brief mention by her friend, Johnston Hastings Skelly, Jr. in a letter to his mother while he was a member of the Union army in Virginia. In the correspondence, Skelly questioned Jennie's conduct, specifically, her "keeping comp [company] so late...." Jennie's response was to deny that she was out late but did not deny that she had company. Skelly continued to his mother, "...thier [sic] has somebody being [sic] trying to raise a fuss between us is my honest belief...for I never heard who was going there or what all the talk there was...."

Is there any reader who can claim that at the age of 20 they never talked or visited into the late hours of the evening with someone of the opposite sex? Surely, it's not all that unusual and it certainly does not mean that she was unfaithful or morally corrupt - she could even have been talking about Skelly, if she, in fact, did have a late visitor to her mother's house.

The stories covering Jennie's character that can be recorded, dated and attributed to fact or at least good sources are all about how at a very early she worked as a seamstress so she could help her mother sustain their home; how she fought to maintain a normal family life despite a father who was branded a "thief" and "very insane"; how she sewed garments and uniforms for Union soldiers and invited them to attend church service with her; she looked after a six-year-old crippled boarder; Jennie spent endless hours baking loaves of bread and biscuits for soldiers and never charged a penny even though times were very tough financially for her family; she devotedly corresponded regularly with her boyfriend who accumulated a packet of letters from her; and she was very dedicated to God and her religious rituals. Jennie was very unselfish as demonstrated by the last words her sister heard her say: "If there is anyone in this house that is to be killed today, I hope it is me, as George has that little baby."

It is a sad thing that so many people who visit Gettysburg are not told the real facts about Jennie's hard work, unselfishness and determination to do good during her twenty years, but that they sometimes come away having heard the oft repeated nonsense that she had a "loose" reputation. These unfounded rumors would not have been taken seriously for so many years had the listeners only asked a simple question at the time. And that is, "What is your source?"

Of course, we must not forget to condemn the virtue, honesty and integrity of the 160,000 or so Confederate and Union soldiers, many of whom while fighting valiantly in the ranks for their respected countries, may have held "soiled and blemished" reputations by being sexually active with women at home or in brothels while in the army. That is hardly ever heard, but, naturally, it is fine, for some, to hold forth a "double standard." One only has to look at the instances of venereal disease in the two military forces as recorded by the medical departments of the U.S. and C.S. Armies to be totally shocked at the lack of sexual and moral restraint among soldiers.

APPENDIX III

The Relationship Between Jennie Wade and Jack Skelly

Were Jennie Wade and Jack Skelly actually engaged to be married? Were they serious about each other? Was it only one-sided? Or could they have been very committed to each other and merely were very private about their feelings?

The answer varies with each source:

The *Pittsburgh Gazette Times* of November 9, 1913, stated, "After Skelly's death his brothers, sisters and surviving comrades learned of his intention to claim Jennie as his bride when he got his furlough in the fall." It continued, "When any celebration or event is 'pulled off' in Gettysburg pertaining to the battle, Mrs. Georgia Wade McClellan, ...is a sure homecomer. She was there at the semi-centennial celebration in July. Mrs. McClellan was asked if she knew that Jack and Jennie had plans to marry. 'Not until after her death, but we expected they would be some day. They were very much in love with each other, but not communicative to us.'"

John Warner, sutler for the 87th Pennsylvania, was one of the last persons to see Jack alive. In the same Pittsburgh paper he recalled about Jack: "The boys in the company and I knew he corresponded regularly with Jennie Wade but we did not know of their engagement and intended marriage."

Mary Virginia did not conceal from Jack's mother her feelings of concern for him just a few days before the battle when a very subdued and ill-at-ease Jennie visited Mrs. Skelly. She asked her if she had received any correspondence from Jack as Jennie had not heard from him recently. Mrs. Skelly had not, and assured Jennie that perhaps the mail delivery was irregular and she would hear from Jack in a few days.

Also, the fact that Jennie carried Jack's photograph in her dress pocket wherever she went showed that she held a special fondness for this particular young man she had come to know so well.

And in a letter to his mother Jack clearly indicated that he was seeing Jennie by saying, "...you should of said something to me when I first commenced going there if you did not like it...," a statement he made when his mother told him she had heard that Jennie supposedly had another suitor.

In 1991, it is the McClellan family's belief that Skelly sent a written message to Jennie via Wesley Culp who was to also inform Skelly's mother that he intended to marry Jennie in September when he expected his furlough to come through.

Unfortunately, since the message was not delivered and the participants did not survive, we may never be able to determine just how serious Jennie and Jack were about each other. There are no known definite sources and letters in existence which say enough on the subject. The author tends to believe that their association was probably more serious than extant sources indicate. Many people who were close to Jennie and Jack point toward their having a relationship more close than being just friends.

Perhaps some reader can inform the author of any missing evidence that could be rewritten into an updated version of this book.

This is the actual Confederate 10-pounder "Parrott" type artillery shell which struck and lodged in the McClellan house on July 2, 1863. It was removed from the structure fifteen years later by Ida M. Kitzmiller. In 1931 she prepared the following affidavit:

This is the shell that passed through the roof of the house now known as The Jennie Wade Museum, during the battle of Gettysburg July 1863.

The shell lodged in the over shot above the kitchen door on the south side of the house, and lay there fifteen years, when it was removed by means of opening the end of the over shot and was located by Ida May Kitzmiller (now Mrs. J. I. Mumper) who was then a little girl living in the house with her parents Jacob A. and Anna L. Kitzmiller and sister Anna Louise Kitzmiller.

After going up the ladder at the end of the house, I groped around in the darkness until I located the shell and handed it to my uncle waiting at the top of the ladder.

The shell has been preserved by the family ever since, and is now in my possession.

Mrs. Ida M. (Kitzmiller) Mumper

Dec. 10th 1931.

(Courtesy of Patricia Weaver Newton and Jamie L. Newton of Gettysburg, PA.)

APPENDIX IV

Why Was John Burns Antagonistic Toward Jennie Wade and Others in Gettysburg?

On January 17, 1866, newspaperman Frank Moore of New York City wrote to John Burns, Gettysburg civilian-turned-hero, and asked him if he knew anything about Jennie Wade, "all the particulars of her life, her character and the manner of her death." He said he was preparing a book, *Women of the War,* in which he "proposed to set before the world the noble acts of our loyal women in this war." Burns' reply was written on the same sheet of paper as the letter of inquiry. He wrote:

> I knew Miss Wade very well. The less said about her the better. The story about her loyalty, her being killed while serving Union soldiers, etc., is all of fiction, got up by some sensation correspondent. The only fact in the whole story is that she was killed during the battle in her house by a stray bullet. Charity to her reputation forbids any further remarks. You can refer, if you choose, to C. Wills Esq. - Postmaster Buehler or any loyal citizen for the truth. I could call her a she-rebel.

In the months that closely followed the battle, John Burns repeatedly shared the hero's spotlight with Jennie Wade in a host of newspaper exchanges between the Harrisburg *Telegraph* and the Adams *Sentinel* of Gettysburg. Jealousy probably provoked some of Burns' resentment toward the young girl who had become instantly famous.

Mayor William G. Weaver was a man who knew both Jennie's mother and her sister, and later owned the McClellan house. He said that John Burns' slighting remarks about Jennie were not borne out by the facts as he knew them. Weaver said:

> If John Burns intended to impute that Jennie Wade was not a Union sympathizer, it may have been because she was not one of the throng of young women who gathered to greet the arrival of General Buford's cavalry. [At the time, Jennie was busy altering the uniform of her brother who had just joined the 21st Pennsylvania Cavalry, a patriotic task, indeed.] I have never heard any aspirations cast on Jennie Wade's character....John Burns' opinion might have been the expression of an old, and probably somewhat irascible resident who may or may not have known much of the young girl.

The Philadelphia *North American* of June 29, 1919 featured a story told by Gettysburg resident Mrs. H. (Jane Powers) McDonnell of yet another time when John Burns accused an unlikely person of being a Southern sympathizer. She described:

> We lived on High Street, and one of our neighbors at the other end of the street

was ill with smallpox. Somehow or another Burns got it into his head that this woman was a rebel sympathizer, which was far from being the case, for, like most if not all of our townspeople, she was loyal and true to her own flag. But no one could convince Burns that this woman was not a friend of the rebels.

On June 11, 1975, Elizabeth M. Tangen, Assistant Curator for the Adams County Historical Society, responded to a letter of inquiry about Jennie Wade by writing, "...We have been unable to find any explanation of Burns' animosity except that he was of a cantankerous nature. Also, Jennie's father was a Southerner.... No one that I have asked seems to have heard of anything else being said about Jennie...."

APPENDIX V

The Interesting History of Jennie Wade's First Coffin

In the rush to bury Mary Virginia Wade during those hot July days directly following her death, there was some confusion over the coffin she was initially buried in. Most people agreed that Jennie's coffin had been intended for a Confederate officer but beyond that the facts became a bit scrambled.

A Gettysburg civilian, Mrs. Jacob A. (Anna Garlach) Kitzmiller, told her opinion in the August 23, 1905 issue of the Gettysburg *Compiler:*

> On the night of July Third we were aroused by some soldiers who asked to be allowed to go in the shop where father made coffins. They said General [William] Barksdale had been killed and they wanted to make a coffin for him...and helping themselves to some wood, [they] went to the shop of Daniel Culp near the Court House. They began the coffin that night but the retreat was ordered before it was finished. This coffin was finished later and Jennie Wade was buried in it when first interred.

In the August 23, 1905 issue of the *Compiler* Daniel Culp, who owned a woodworking shop near the Court House, stated, "On the night of July 3rd Confederate soldiers took wood from Henry Garlach's woodworking shop, brought it here and began to make a coffin for Gen. Barksdale. The Confederate retreat began before it was finished. The coffin was finished later and Jennie Wade was buried in it."

In a manuscript he wrote during the last ten years of his life, John C. Will described his version of the story behind the coffin:

> ...on Saturday morning [the Confederates] called upon A prominent citizen and who was A carpenter and contractor to secure a coffin and have it brought out and have the body placed into it preparatory for burial. Now there was A prominent citizen who was a prominent manufacturer and dealer in Furniture and whose residence and Furniture shop was situated on Baltimore st. south of and adjoining the Court House. the carpenter went to him and asked permission to go to his shop and make A coffin. his request was granted....A number of confederates...took possession of this Furniture shop and were making coffins to place their dead into now those confederates had cut out A coffin of walnut wood for the purpose of placing into it the body of A North Carolina Confederate Col. or Gen. to be shipped to his home. those confederates inexpectedly to them, being compelled to retreat on Friday night this coffin was left in its rough and unfinished state the carpenter going into the shop and Looking around for material he came across this unfinished walnut coffin. he took it dressed up the material [and] completed the job. he took it out to the House and placed into it the body of Jennie Wade. they then took her to the rear of the House and buried her in the Garden....

The dead Confederate officer was probably not General Barksdale, who died and was buried at a Union field hospital at Jacob Hummelbaugh's house on the Taneytown Road. Most likely this was Isaac E. Avery, acting brigade commander and colonel of the 6th North Carolina Infantry who was mortally wounded on the evening of July 2, leading Hoke's brigade in a charge up East Cemetery Hill.

The only other possible higher-ranking Confederate officers who died in any area near the village were Lieutenant Colonel Michael Nolan, 1st Louisiana Infantry of Nicholl's Brigade and Colonel Trevanion D. Lewis, 8th Louisiana Infantry of Hay's Brigade, both of whom were killed near Culp's Hill on Thursday, July 2.

APPENDIX VI

The Fatal Shot - From Where and By Whom?

Amidst all of the confusion as the battle was raging, it was, of course, impossible to know who fired the shot that killed Jennie Wade.

It is most likely that soon after her death, concerned and curious people studied the angle of the bullet holes in the two doors and the rise of three-and-one-half inches between them. Those with inquisitive minds stood at the doors and lined up the angle of the shot and deducted that the bullet must have come from the west side of Baltimore Street, somewhere near the intersection of the Emmitsburg Road, in all probability, from a building at the John Rupp Tannery. Then, there seems to be evidence that several Louisiana Infantry companies were positioned in the southern part of the borough on both sides of Baltimore Street, in the houses of Harvey D. Sweney, Samuel McCreary, John Rupp, and others. Lieutenant Henry E. Handerson of the 9th Louisiana wrote many years after the battle: "...the main street,...was swept by the bullets of the enemy's skirmishers...at each of the front windows a couple of men were occasionally exchanging shots with the enemy...we scampered to the shelter of another house, still nearer the enemy, behind which I found half-a-dozen comrades skirmishing with a force of the enemy a short distance below."

Although the evidence is not perfectly clear, it seems most probable that, considering the position and angle of the bullet holes and the existence of sharpshooters located in the direction from whence the shots came, the fatal shot that killed Jennie Wade came from around the John Rupp Tannery, fired by a Louisiana rifleman.

APPENDIX VII

Where Was Wesley Culp Buried?

On the evening of July 3, B.S. Pendleton, an orderly with the Stonewall Brigade, told Wesley's sisters the sad news of Culp's death. He soon left their home after minutely describing the burial spot as he had taken pains to remember it. Wesley was supposedly buried under a crooked tree on Culp's Hill, his grave plainly marked. Wesley's sisters, Annie and Julia searched for their brother's grave along with uncles and cousins, but all looked in vain for the body. They found dozens of broken trees and lots of bodies under them, but they never found Wesley. They were able only to find the stock of a rifle with the words "W. Culp" carved on it.

What should be remembered at this juncture was the extreme bitterness of most of the people of Gettysburg against the Rebels. Taking this into consideration, some people find it reasonable to assume that Culp's family may have found his body and decided, secretly, to leave it buried there on Culp's Hill, to avoid any expressions of anger in the community over the fact that Culp had fought for the Southern army. Just imagine what would have happened if the surviving relatives had asked permission for his remains to be buried in the Evergreen Cemetery with his father and mother or in the Methodist churchyard with his brothers and sisters? The "pot would have boiled over" for Wesley Culp was a native who had betrayed his own people. If his family did leave him right there on Culp's Hill, he at least had a quiet and peaceful resting place, outside of the bounds of controversy.

The truth of the matter is, that Culp's grave like so many others, was simply lost through the ravages of time and the elements. In fact, on this section of the field, most of the Confederates were interred by Federal soldiers who marked few, if any, enemy graves.

APPENDIX VIII

John White Johnston

John White Johnston was one of the first people to recognize the significance of Mary Virginia Wade's story. Some time around 1910, at the age of 31, this avid student of the Civil War, traveled to Gettysburg to do a thorough study of Jennie Wade and John Burns. Johnston gave lectures and published numerous papers and several pamphlets on the "Hero and Heroine" of Gettysburg.

At the 50th Anniversary Celebration of the Battle of Gettysburg, John White Johnston met Georgia Wade McClellan who agreed to furnish him with information and materials pertaining to her sister's life and death. In 1917, a publication entitled *The True Story of "Jennie" Wade, A Gettysburg Maid*, was written and published by J.W. Johnston in Rochester, New York and dedicated to Mary Ann Filby Wade, Jennie's mother. Almost forty pages long, it contained family accounts and photographs acquired through Georgia. No one else had spent so much time and money to capture Jennie's true story as Johnston did at a time when some of her closest family members were still alive to give probably the most accurate accounts as will ever be given.

Johnston also gathered a collection of relics pertaining to Jennie's life and death. Fascinated with her story, this native of Rochester, purchased Jennie's birthplace in 1950 on Baltimore Street and the Wade family's Breckenridge Street home in 1920. His intent was to sell the booklets from these locations while having her mementos on display, reaping great profits of which he intended to send to Georgia. His dream never came true, probably because Robert C. Miller had the same idea at the McClellan house where he initially sold the booklets and had exhibits in what became known as the "Jennie Wade House" Museum. For some reason, though, Miller discontiued the sale of the books there, which greatly provoked both Johnston and Mrs. McClellan. Georgia then attempted to retrieve the original mixing tray she had given to Miller in hopes of handing it over to Johnston. Although he made a very aggressive attempt over a period of several years, which included the financing of two trips for Mrs. McClellan to travel from Iowa to Gettysburg, Johnston was never successful at owning that dough tray as a part of his collection.

He did, according to correspondence with a local liaison, J. Lewis Sowers of Harrisburg, attempt to publish later editions of the booklet. In a September 12, 1927 letter to Sowers, Johnston invited him to help prepare copy for a second edition which this author can not find was ever updated.

In her final years, Georgia McClellan asked J.W. Johnston to work with the appropriate authorities to have her sister's monument inscription changed from "Jennie" to "Ginnie" or to "Mary Virginia Wade," a request that was never completed. Perhaps Johnston saw this as the desire of a woman in her last years to "right all wrongs." In this case, the wrong had been one of her doings, since she

70

was actively instrumental in the design of that monument and the manner in which the name appeared.

John White Johnston graduated from Harvard University in 1905 and from the Harvard School of Law in 1907. Upon graduation, he was employed in the advertising department of Sibley, Lindsay and Curr Company, which, co-founded by his father and two other partners, became the largest retail store between New York and Chicago.

This Harvard graduate was listed in Rochester's Who's Who as: manufacturer, author, lecturor, composer, historian, corporate executive, publisher, botanist, artist, inventor and philanthropist.

As the author of the new "Jennie Wade Story," I must extend a special thanks to this man of many talents, for a great part of my book was built upon the facts that he diligently collected from sources who can not be interviewed today.

Civil War era envelopes believed to have been addressed in the handwriting of Jennie Wade and Jack Skelly prior to their untimely deaths in 1863. (Courtesy of Patricia Weaver Newton and Jamie L. Newton of Gettysburg, PA.)

Notes to Appendices

Other Civilian Losses During and After the Battle of Gettysburg:
Gregory A. Coco. *A Vast Sea of Misery, A History and Guide to the Union and Confederate Field Hospitals at Gettysburg, July 1- November 20, 1863,* Thomas Publications, Gettysburg, PA, 1988, p. 65.
Gregory A. Coco. *On The Bloodstained Field,* Thomas Publications, Gettysburg, PA, 1987, p. 9, 47.
Robert K. Krick, *The Confederate Death Roster,* July 1-3, 1863, Morningside Bookshop, Dayton, OH, 1981, p. 44.
Miscellaneous Civilian Accounts File, Mary McAllister Account, GNMP Library.
The Gettysburg Times, Centennial Edition, 1963.

The Moral Factor in Determining the Reputation of Mary Virginia Wade:
Johnston H. Skelly, Jr. letter dated April 7, 1863, to Elizabeth F. Skelly, located in pension file at National Archives.

The Relationship Between Jennie Wade and Jack Skelly:
Letter from Johnston Hastings Skelly, Jr. to his mother, Elizabeth F. Skelly, in pension file at National Archives.
Conversation with Deah Schwarzenbach Bruhn, great-granddaughter of Georgia Wade McClellan.

Why Was John Burns Antagonistic Toward Jennie Wade and Others in Gettysburg?
The Gettysburg Times Centennial Edition, 1963.
The Wade family file at Adams County Historical Society.

The Interesting History of Jennie Wade's First Coffin:
The Gettysburg *Compiler,* August 23, 1905.
John C. Will, "Reminiscences of the Three Days Battle of Gettysburg at the Globe Hotel," manuscript in the GNMP Library.

The Fatal Shot - From Where and By Whom?
Henry E. Handerson. *Yankee in Gray.* The Press of Western Reserve University, 1962, p. 63.

Where Was Wesley Culp Buried?
The Gettysburg Times, November 16, 1978.
The Pittsburgh Gazette Times, November 9, 1913.

John White Johnston:
Walter L. Powell, Ph.D., owner of a collection of letters between John White Johnston and J. Louis Sowers of the Auditor General's Office in Harrisburg, PA, from November 13, 1919 to September 12, 1927.
J.W. Johnston File in Adams County Historical Society.
Historic Building Survey Committee #168-89, Adams County Historical Society.

Notes

Special thanks to John White Johnston, author of *The True Story of "Jennie" Wade, A Gettysburg Maid*, written in 1917. A great part of my book was built upon the facts he diligently collected from sources who cannot be interviewed today.

When more than one footnote occurred within the same paragraph, the author listed all of the sources in order as they appear all under one footnote notation at the end of the paragraph for ease of reading.

[1] The verses that open each chapter are from the following poems: "Jenny Wade of Gettysburg" by Mary H. Eastman, J.B. Lippincott Company, Philadelphia, PA, 1864; and "The Maid of Gettysburg," in the Gettysburg *Compiler*, July 22, 1903.

[2] The 1860 Borough of Gettysburg Census lists Samuel and Elizabeth Filby as living just yards away from the McClellan house near the Wagon Hotel, only their name was mistakenly registered as "Philbee" not Filby. At that time, Samuel S. Wade, 10 years old, was recorded as living in their home. Census located at Adams County Historical Society, Gettysburg, PA, hereinafter referred to as ACHS.

Mary Ann Filby was James Wade's second wife. Wade and his first wife, whose last name was Kuntz, had one child, James A. Wade, born on February 27, 1839 near Gettysburg. In 1861 this son enlisted in the 3rd Pennsylvania Heavy Artillery, in which he became a corporal; he was stationed at Fort Monroe, VA, during the Battle of Gettysburg. He married Lavina Weaner on February 25, 1869 in Bendersville, PA, and moved to Manchester, Kansas in Dickinson County. They had no children, but adopted a daughter, Bertic. James died on December 29, 1915 in Manchester. Source in McClellan family file at ACHS.

The death of Martha Margaret Culp was recorded in the Gettysburg *Compiler* on September 17, 1849.

It is interesting to note that during the year that Harry was conceived, James Wade, Sr. was a resident of the Adams County Poor House and listed as "very insane."

There has been some confusion as to whether Jennie's true birthdate was May 21 or 26, 1843. Sources that list May 21, 1843 are *The True Story of Jennie Wade* which Georgia Wade supplied most of the information for, and, the tablet that marks her birthplace that was unveiled by Georgia reads May 21, 1843. However, various letters to researchers written by Elizabeth M. Tangen, assistant director of the ACHS in 1976 list her date of birth as both May 21 and May 26, and the Trinity Reformed Church burial files place her birthdate as May 26, 1843. The author believes Georgia's references should prove to be correct as May 21. All of these sources list the year as 1843 which made her 20 years old at the time of her death.

Wade family file at ACHS.

John White Johnston. *The True Story of "Jennie" Wade, A Gettysburg Maid.* 1917. J.W. Johnston, p. 5. Hereinafter cited as "John White Johnston."

[3] The October 9, 1985 issue of *The Gettysburg Times* shows Jennie's birthplace at 242-246 Baltimore Street when it was restored by Randall and Martha Inskip. An historic architect hired by the Inskips surmised that the house was built sometime between 1814 and 1820 and a back addition housing a kitchen was added around 1870. The Wades never owned this house according to tax records. (During the battle it was owned by Peter Frey.) On April 3, 1920, J. W. Johnston, author of *The True Story of "Jennie" Wade*, bought her birthplace for

$3,800 and sold it on June 5, 1950 for $6,750 according to Deed Book 88, p. 161, and Deed Book, 191, p. 58, respectively. Information supplied by Elwood W. Christ.

[4] According to some Gettysburg battle historians, Mary Virginia Wade's nickname was Ginny, not Jennie or Jenny. In all these years, though, the family still believes that she was "Jennie" as was used by her sister, Georgia, her mother, Mary Wade in her will and her boyfriend, Johnston Hastings Skelly, Jr. in a letter to his mother. Sources are Georgia's great-grandson, Kenneth Wade Schwarzenbach; Mary Wade's will in ACHS Wade file; Skelly's letter in the National Archives in his pension file.

[5] Circa 1853 tax records indicate that George Schryock transferred a 1/2 lot to Mary Ann Wade who erected a house either late that year or before the fall of 1854. A cursory exterior survey suggests that the original dwelling was rectangular, that a back building and the east addition were added, and finally a rear structure which resulted in the current square configuration. Mary Wade retained the property until her death in 1892. Found in Gettysburg Historic Building Survey Committee (HBSC) File #168-89, originals in PA Historical & Museum Commission, Bureau for Historical Preservation, and copies in ACHS files.
It is the Schwarzenbach family's belief in 1991 that James Wade Sr.'s illness was diabetes, a disease which exists within the family.

[6] Samuel Durboraw farmed 100 acres about a mile northeast of the village of Two Taverns at the time of the Battle of Gettysburg.
Adams *Sentinel,* September 2, 1850.
Paper written by John S. Patterson, Philadelphia, PA, October 19, 1989, in Jennie Wade file at Gettysburg National Military Park Library, hereinafter cited as GNMP Library.
The Eastern State Penitentiary which opened in 1829 was located in Philadelphia as stated in *The Cradle of the Penitentiary, The Walnut Street Jail at Philadelphia, 1773-1835* by Negley K. Teeters, Temple University, sponsored by the Pennsylvania Prison Society, 1955, printed in U.S.A., p. 123.

[7] Adams County Court of Common Pleas, Appearance and Judgment Docket, Col. W (1851-53), p. 81-83.
1860 and 1870 Cumberland Township Census at ACHS lists James Wade, Sr. as a "pauper" who was "very insane."

[8] John White Johnston, op cit., p. 7.
Denison Review, May, 1917, Iowa newspaper article entitled, "Georgia Wade McClellan's Part in the Civil War."
Carroll, Iowa newspaper, September 2, 1927.
Gettysburg *Star and Sentinel,* June 4, 1889.
Thirty years after John Louis McClellan was born, his father had a second son to Martha Richardson, whom he also did not marry. It is interesting that the *History of Cumberland and Adams Counties, 1886,* Adams Section, Chicago: Warner, Beers & Co., p. 362, states: "He [Colonel John Joseph H. McClellan] has never married," which is preceded with "Mr. McClellan is identified with the Presbyterian Church, and is highly esteemed for his excellent qualities." It also said, "For 150 years the family name of McClellan has been a familiar one to...[Adams County], and is widely respected and honored."
Samuel P. Bates. *History of Pennsylvania Volunteers, 1861-5.* Harrisburg, B. Singerly, state printer, 1869-71, p. 1092, hereinafter cited as "Samuel P. Bates."

John Louis and Georgia McClellan first moved to Mahaska County, Iowa, where "Louis" was a carpenter for about one year. They later moved to Denison, Iowa where Louis worked as a building contractor with his friend, H.C. Laub, building many large structures throughout Crawford County, including the "old courthouse" and the "west brick school building" in the county seat of Denison. In 1911, Louis and Georgia moved to Fort Dodge, Iowa, to take charge of the Benedict Home, a rescue mission for unwed mothers. It was there, at 6:30 p.m. on March 4, 1913, in the company of his wife and his son, "J.B." (James Britton), that John Louis McClellan died.

Another source used was geneological research done by family, given to the author by Deah Schwarzenbach Bruhn, great-granddaughter of John Louis McClellan.

[9] John White Johnston, op. cit., p. 7.

[10] Herbert L. Grim and Paul L. Roy. *Human Interest Stories of the THREE DAYS' BATTLES AT GETTYSBURG with Pictures*. Times News Publishing Co., Gettysburg, PA, 1927, p. 24.

[11] John Wesley Culp file, GNMP Library.

[12] *Pittsburgh Gazette Times*, November 9, 1913, Section 5, p. 3.
Charles William Hoffman and his three sons also joined the Confederate Army as cited in the Miscellaneous Civilian Accounts file at GNMP Library.

[13] Ibid.

[14] Ibid.
Samuel P. Bates, op. cit.: William Culp, p. 33; William Holtzworth, p. 47; Charles Edwin Skelly, p. 51; Johnston H. Skelly, Jr., p. 50; Johnston H. Skelly, Sr., p. 631; William Ziegler, p. 50.

[15] *The Gettysburg Times*, April 28, 1973.

[16] Ibid.

[17] *Pittsburgh Gazette Times*, November 9, 1913, Section 5, p.3.

[18] Ibid.
The Gettysburg Times, April 28, 1973.

[19] John White Johnston, op. cit., p. 7. Jennie's uncle, Thaddeus Filby, became a member of Company M of the 21st PA Volunteer Cavalry in February of 1864. He received a gunshot wound to the head at Petersburg, VA on June 18, 1864 and died as a result on March 31, 1865 at the age of 35. A resident of the Gettysburg borough, Filby left behind a wife, Harriet, 32, and two young daughters. He was buried beside his niece, Mary Virginia Wade. Found in McClellan family file in ACHS.

[20] Lydia Catherine (Ziegler) Clare, "A Gettysburg Girl's Story," unpublished manuscript dated "about 1900," ACHS files.
Sarah M. Broadhead. *The Diary of a Lady of Gettysburg, PA, from June 15 to July 15, 1863,* privately printed, in typescript at ACHS, hereinafter cited as "Sarah M. Broadhead."
Michael Jacobs. *Notes on the Rebel Invasion of Maryland and Pennsylvania and the Battle of Gettysburg.* Philadelphia: J.B. Lippincott & Co., 1864.

[21] Robert F. McClean, "A Boy at Gettysburg in 1863," Gettysburg *Compiler,* June 30, 1909. Gates D. Fahnestock, "Speech Before the National Arts Club of New York, February 14, 1934." Hereinafter cited as Gates D. Fahnestock. Both a printed and a handwritten copy of Fahnestock's remarks are on file at the ACHS.

[22] Newspaper article from Carroll, Iowa, dated September 2, 1927, entitled, "She Served at Gettysburg."
The McClellan family, today, claims the child's name was "Louis" not "Lewis" as it incorrectly appeared in several newspaper accounts.

[23] Samuel P. Bates, op. cit., shows him as a private, enlisted June 23, 1863, transferred to Co. B, 182nd PA Volunteers (3 yrs. reg.), Feb. 1, 1864.
John White Johnston, op. cit., p. 8.

[24] Matilda (Tillie) Pierce Alleman. *At Gettysburg or What a Girl Saw and Heard of the Battle. A True Narrative.* New York, W. Lake Borland, 1889, p. 5. Hereinafter cited as "Matilda Pierce Alleman."

[25] John White Johnston, op. cit., p. 9.
The Gettysburg Times, January 20, 1958, "William G. Weaver Speaks to Civil War Round Table.
Matilda Pierce Alleman, op. cit., p. 5, 6. Matilda or "Tillie's" version was quite different from Johnston's. In her account she says Jennie held her family responsible for her brother's safety by yelling at her (Matilda's) mother, "If the rebs take Sam, I don't know what I'll do with you folks!" Matilda claimed that when her father went before the Confederate commander to retrieve the horse that he was refused because he was a "Black Abolitionist; so black, that he was turning black;" a bit of information that Matilda accused Jennie of relaying to the Southern officer. Miss Pierce said, "....I am afraid her sympathies were not so much for the Union as they should have been."

[26] John C. Will, "Reminiscences of the Three Days Battle of Gettysburg at the Globe Hotel," manuscript in the GNMP Library. Hereinafter cited as "John C. Will."
Samuel P. Bates. *Martial Deeds of Pennsylvania.* T.H. Davis & Co., Philadelphia, PA, 1876, p. 1082.
Gates D. Fahnestock, op. cit.
Leonard H. Gardner, "Sunset Memories," *The Gettysburg Times,* September 10, 1940. In 1863, York Springs was called "Petersburg," but by the time this account was written it was known as "York Springs."

[27] John White Johnston, op. cit., p. 13.

[28] Ibid, p. 13.

[29] Albertus McCreary, *McClure's* magazine, July 1909, p. 245.
The Gettysburg *Compiler,* June 29, 1863.
Sarah M. Broadhead, op. cit.
Abner Doubleday. *Chancellorsville and Gettysburg: Campaigns of the Civil War,* 6 vols. New York: Charles Scribner's Sons 1882, 6:149.

[30] John C. Will, op. cit.
Anna Garlach Kitzmiller, "Mrs. Kitzmiller's Story," Gettysburg *Compiler,* August 23, 1905. Hereinafter cited as "Anna Garlach Kitzmiller."

[31] Gettysburg *Compiler,* December 28, 1897.
Samuel P. Bates, op. cit., p. 912.

[32] Philadelphia *Public Ledger and Daily Transcript,* September 16, 1901, entitled, "Iowa Women Honor Gettysburg Heroine." It is most likely that this house was used by Union soldiers as a hideout but these men probably did not fire their weapons since that action would draw fire at the residents also in the building.

[33] Miscellaneous Civilian Accounts File, GNMP Library. The soldier killed was Private William Poole, 9th Louisiana Infantry.
1860 Gettysburg Borough Census in ACHS.

[34] Historic Building Survey Committee File #168-89 in ACHS files.

[35] Ibid.
A November 29, 1863 letter from Henry Sweney, Harvey's son, to Andrew, another son, shows they spelled their name as "Sweney." Letter in Gregory A. Coco files.
In 1991 the Sweney house is known as the Historic Farnsworth House which features a restaurant, inn and museum. Over 100 bullet holes can still be seen in the house today. In July of 1863, a bullet shattered an upstairs window and lodged in the bedpost as cited in the Historic Farnsworth House brochure, 1991.

[36] John White Johnston, op. cit., p. 15.

[37] Ibid, op. cit., p. 15.

[38] The Wade family file at the ACHS features a document that said: "There were here at the Fiftieth Anniversary Union soldiers who said they fired from in front of the 'Jennie Wade House' seventy rounds at the Confederates at the Tannery Buildings without stopping." *Star and Sentinel,* September 25, 1901.

[39] John White Johnston, op. cit., p. 19, lists Mrs. Catharine McClain as "McLean" and mentions she had five children during the battle. In the October 19, 1952 issue of the *Baltimore Sun,* Susan McClain, one of those children, goes by "McClain" and mentions she had three brothers and sisters making the number of children to total four. The October 30, 1915 issue of the *Compiler* lists the name spelled "McClain." The 1860 census at the ACHS lists the family name as "McClaine."

The same October edition of the *Baltimore Sun* indicated that Mrs. McClain and her children were hiding in the basement with the Wade family and Jennie's corpse. Susan McClain remembered that at the time Jennie was killed the McClains had been living in the basement since the moment the shell hit their house. In the same vein, the January 20, 1958 *Gettysburg Times* described William G. Weaver, owner of the McClellan house at that time, telling the Gettysburg Civil War Round Table that "The McClain family took to the cellar on their side....Jennie's family went down the stairway on the McClain side, and in that fashion reached the cellar on the McClain side of the house where all remained until after the battle had ended." In contradiction, a letter in the Wade file at the ACHS from the Historical Society states that "the family on that side had left."

[40] *The Gettysburg Times*, April 28, 1973, reports that John Wesley Culp visited his sickly mother during the battle, which was impossible since she died on November 7, 1856 of dropsy of the chest, according to the Wade file at the ACHS.
Pittsburgh Gazette Times, November 9, 1913, Section 5, p. 3.

[41] Ibid.
The Gettysburg Times, April 28, 1973.
Ashley Halsey, Jr. *Who Fired The First Shot?* First Crest Printing, Fawcett World Library, New York, N.Y., December 1963, p. 196.
Evergreen Cemetery Burial Permit in Wade family file at ACHS.

[42] *Pittsburgh Gazette Times*, November 9, 1913, Section 5, p. 3.

[43] Culp family file at ACHS.
The November 9, 1913 *Pittsburgh Gazette Times* claims that John Wesley Culp was killed July 2nd, but two eyewitness accounts (Douglas and Casler), plus Culp's military records in the National Archives signed by his company commander, state that he was killed early on July 3rd. Also, Walker's Brigade was more heavily engaged on the 3rd, hence it was more likely that Culp met his death at that time. Therefore, the author believes John Wesley Culp was killed on July 3rd.
Henry Kyd Douglas. *I Rode With Stonewall.* Chapel Hill: The University of North Carolina Press, 1940. p. 251.
John O. Casler. *Four Years in the Stonewall Brigade.* Dayton, Ohio: Morningside Bookshop, 1971, p. 182.

[44] John White Johnston, op. cit., p. 21.

[45] Ibid, p. 21.

[46] Ibid, p. 21.

[47] Ibid, p. 23.
When Mary Wade died in 1892, Georgia McClellan inherited the mixing tray which she took with her when she moved to Iowa. In 1991, the author spoke to her great-grandson, Kenneth Wade Schwarzenbach, 77, who said he clearly remembers using the mixing tray as a toybox as a child until he was eight years old. Georgia then donated the wooden box to the Jennie Wade Museum. According to Mary Ann Filby Wade's last will and testament located in the Wade family file at ACHS, Georgia also inherited the bedstead she used during the battle, the coffee mill, and a framed picture of Jennie. Mr. Schwarzenbach also noted that his family has a Minie' ball that Georgia found in her yard when the fighting was over. In 1991, Deah Schwarzenbach Bruhn told the author that Georgia McClellan claimed that Jennie was not standing over the mixing tray which was on the other side of the kitchen, instead, she was kneading the biscuit mixture in a dough bowl made of light maple wood, 18" long by 12" wide and 6" deep, a rectangular shape with the center scooped out. Georgia gave the dough bowl to her granddaughter, Georgia Wade Schwarzenbach who gave it to her son, Kenneth Wade Schwarzenbach. The wooden kitchen table upon which Jennie sat the bowl was later made into a desk which is now owned by Gretchen Triplett, Kenneth

Schwarzenbach's niece in Iowa.

[48] According to the Schwarzenbach family, Georgia Wade McClellan said the fatal bullet penetrated the doorknob section of the door and struck Jennie.

[49] John White Johnston, op. cit., p. 25.

[50] Ibid, p. 25.

At the age of 85, Johnston H. Skelly, Jr.'s sister, Anne, recalled the photograph in her "Recollections of the Battle of Gettysburg" dated December 8, 1941, in the Skelly family file at ACHS. It said, "Miss Annie Skelly is the owner of the picture of Corp. Johnston Skelly that was in the pocket of Jennie Wade at the time she was killed in the Battle. This is the only picture of its kind and therefore original." A larger photograph of Skelly is still located in the G.A.R. Post No.9 building on East Middle Street in Gettysburg.

The purse carried by Jennie on the day of her death is now on display in the Christian C. Sanderson Museum in Chadds Ford, PA. In 1913 Christian Sanderson, a lifelong collector of mementos, traveled to Gettysburg for the 50th Anniversary of the battle. He encountered Georgia Wade McClellan there for the first time and soon afterward a package from her arrived from Iowa which contained the purse Jennie was carrying in her apron the day she was killed. The purse and a 1913 photo of Georgia taken by Mr. Sanderson were featured in an article about him and his museum in the January 21, 1991 issue of *Insight* magazine. Special thanks to Thomas R. Thompson and the Christian C. Sanderson Museum for the use of these photos and to Merlin and Lucy Coco for bringing the reference to my attention.

[51] James Stuart Montgomery. *The Shaping of a Battle: Gettysburg*. Chilton Company-Book Division, Philadelphia & New York, 1959. p. 136.

[52] Sarah M. Broadhead, op. cit.

[53] George R. Stewart. *Pickett's Charge, July 3, 1863*. The Riverside Press. Houghton Mifflin Company. Cambridge, MA, 1959, Foreword.

[54] William Hamilton Bayly, "Memoir of a Thirteen-Year-Old Boy," in files of ACHS.

[55] Daniel Skelly, "A Boy's Experience During the Battle of Gettysburg," Gettysburg, PA, 1932, in Skelly family file at ACHS.
Robert F. McLean, op. cit.

[56] Matilda Pierce Alleman, op. cit.

[57] Reverend Dr. Jacobs, "Meteorology of the Battle," for the Gettysburg *Star and Sentinel*, in GNMP files.
John White Johnston, op. cit., p. 27.
McClellan family file at ACHS.

[58] John White Johnston, op. cit., p. 25.

[59] James Stuart Montgomery, op. cit., p. 188. This quote implies the possibility that Jennie's younger brother, Samuel, may have attended her funeral, having come from where he stayed during the battle, at the home of James Pierce, nearly five hundred yards away.

[60] Conversation with great-grandchildren of Georgia McClellan, Kenneth Wade Schwarzenbach and Deah Schwarzenbach Bruhn of Carroll, Iowa, February, 1991.

[61] John White Johnston, op. cit., p. 28.
The Occasional Writings of Isaac Moorhead with a Sketch of His Life, by A.H. Caughey, published by A.H. Caughey, 1882, in GNMP files. Isaac Moorhead recorded that in October of 1864 he visited Gettysburg's Evergreen Cemetery and noted Jennie Wade's grave there. He said, "In passing through we saw a stone with this inscription: 'Be ye ready! Jennie Wade, killed by a ball fired by a Rebel sharpshooter at the Battle of Gettysburg, July 3d, 1863, whilst in discharge of her household duties.'"

[62] The U.S. Christian Commission's Annual Report severely criticized Burns' unruly actions because they disrupted the Commission's operations which had been disarranged, rendering them less systematic and orderly than elsewhere since Reverend Alexander could not perform his duties for quite some time. This, however, was not Burns' first brush with the law. During his military career he was brought up on charges for misconduct three times, but never cashiered. The rowdy Irishman was mustered out at the end of the Civil War as a lieutenant colonel and lived his last years as harbor master in New York City where he died on December 7, 1883.
Gregory A. Coco. *On The Bloodstained Field*, Vol. II, Thomas Publications, Gettysburg, PA, 1989, p. 83.
Edmund J. Raus, Jr. *A Generation on the March - The Union Army at Gettysburg.* H.E. Howard, Inc., Lynchburg, VA, 1987, p. 70.
U.S. Christian Commission for the Army and Navy Work and Incidents, First Annual Report, Philadelphia, PA, February, 1863, p. 74,

[63] *Harper's* Magazine, "Four Days at Gettysburg," February, 1864, p. 387.

[64] Robert S. Robertson. *Diary of the War 1861-4.* Edited by Charles and Rosemary Walker, in files of Gregory A. Coco.

[65] For years it was believed that this nameless heroine was some other unfortunate woman killed in action at Gettysburg. The author believes that it is a corruption of the true events of Jennie Wade's death. Gettysburg was a small town, with most of the people very aware of the goings on there. Another female civilian's death would have undoubtedly been recorded by the family, a neighbor, etc. and even a woman traveling through to nurse the wounded would have been mentioned by at least a handful of witnesses in such a situation. Also, it was obvious through the words, "as the wounded soldiers came hobbling by," that the woman was shot as they retreated southward which was near the location of the McClellan House. Also, the 76th New York Volunteers were deployed on the northeast slope near the top of Culp's Hill on July 2 and 3. Their retreat from the "unfinished railroad cut" area late on July 1 to Culp's Hill took the remnants of the regiment directly past where Jennie Wade was handing out water.

[66] *Baltimore Sun*, October 16, 1952 depicts Susan McClain's recollection eighty-nine years later when she traveled to the McClellan dwelling during the 100th anniversary of the Western Maryland Railroad.

[67] Gettysburg *Compiler*, July 26, 1905, "A Woman's Thrilling Experiences of the Battle, by

Elizabeth Thorn," p. 2.

[58] Miscellaneous Civilian Accounts file at GNMP Library.

[59] *The Arbor State*, a newspaper dated May 30, 1944, in Wymore, Nebraska.

[70] Sophronia E. Bucklin. I*n Hospital and Camp: A Woman's Record of Thrilling Incidents Among the Wounded in the Late War.* John E. Potter and Company, Philadelphia, PA, 1869.

[71] Mary Warren Fastnacht. *Memories of the Battle of Gettysburg, Year 1863.* Princely Press, Inc. New York, NY, August, 1941.

[72] Miscellaneous Civilian Accounts file at GNMP Library.
Also mentioning that the bullet passed through a window was Albertus McCreary in *McClure's*, op. cit. He said, "....she was shot by a stray bullet that came through an open window and struck her in the breast....she had lived in our family and was personally well known to us all...."

[73] *Pittsburgh Gazette Times*, November 9, 1913, Section 5, p. 3.

[74] Used as a temporary field hospital after the battle, the Methodist Church, later the G.A.R. Post, became a gathering point for visiting veterans and their families, especially during the 25th Anniversary of the Battle. Currently, it serves as the meetingplace of the local chapter of the Sons of Union Veterans, the Gettysburg Civil War Round Table, and The Gettysburg Battlefield Preservation Association. Historic Building Survey Committee File # 163-89, ACHS files.
John White Johnston, op, cit., p. 33.

[5] U.S. Civil War Nurses Association, Gregory A. Coco files.

[6] Article entitled, "Georgia Wade McClellan's Part in the Civil War" May 1917 issue of *Denison Review,* Iowa newspaper.
Article entitled, "Woman Writes of Famous Battle," May 8, 1917 issue of D*es Moines Register.*

[7] Carroll, Iowa newspaper dated September 2, 1927.

[8] *The Gettysburg Times,* June 3, 1968.
Conversation with Kenneth Wade Schwarzenbach, great-grandson of Georgia McClellan, February, 1991.
1927 Iowa newspaper article with dateline listed as Carroll, Iowa, September 2, 1927, entitled, "She Served at Gettysburg, Civil War Nurse, Memory Dimming, Waits 'Taps' in Hospital at Carroll, Ia." This article appeared just five days before Georgia died.
John White Johnston, op. cit., p. 2.

[*] The May of 1917 *Denison Review* newspaper said that in her last days Georgia wrote a letter to Oscar Woodruff, one of the few survivors of the 10th New York Cavalry, "....The old soldiers hold the first place in my thoughts, and especially those on the field of Gettysburg." In one incident when her memory wandered back to the stirring days of her youth, she said to her hospital nurse, "There's a boy across the hall who wants a letter written to his mother.

He's wounded so bad he'll never live. I do wish you'd write it for him." Conversation with Georgia's great-grandson, Kenneth Wade Schwarzenbach, Carroll, Iowa, February, 1991.

[80] *The Gettysburg Times,* December 5, 1949, John's daughter, Nellie Virginia Wade Coston, says he told her he delivered a message to President Lincoln as he sat on the platform on November 19, 1863, prior to the delivery of his immortal address.
The Gettysburg Times, January 10, 1953, says his son, John, while visiting Gettysburg, recalled his father telling the story of Jennie altering his uniform on June 26, 1863.
Historic Building Survey Committee File # 168-89.
McClellan family file at ACHS.

[81] Wade and McClellan family files at ACHS.
Gettysburg *Compiler,* November 26, 1869.
1870 Gettysburg Borough Census, ACHS files.

[82] *Sierro Gordo County Republican*, Mason City newspaper, January 3, 1901.
McClellan family file at ACHS.

[83] 1860, 1870 Cumberland Township Census for Adams County Alms House or Poor House, at ACHS.
McClellan family file at ACHS.
Gettysburg *Star and Sentinel*, July 11, 1872.

[84] *The Gettysburg Times,* "Seventy-five Years Ago" column, 1955.
The Gettysburg Times, April 28, 1921.
1860 Gettysburg Borough Census, ACHS.

[85] Wade and McClellan family files at ACHS.
Historic Building Survey Committee File # 168-89.
1870 Gettysburg Borough Census in ACHS files.

[86] *The Gettysburg Times,* February 13, 1941.
Conversation with his namesake, Kenneth Wade Schwarzenbach, Carroll, Iowa, February, 1991.
McClellan family file at ACHS.

[87] *Sierro Gordo County Republican,* Mason City, Iowa, January 3, 1901.
Carroll, Iowa newspaper dated September 2, 1927.

[88] Wade family file at ACHS.
Gettysburg *Star and Sentinel,* September 11 and 25, 1901.

[89] Gettysburg *Star and Sentinel,* September 11, 1901.

[90] John White Johnston, op. cit., p. 29.

[91] *The Gettysburg Times,* February 21, 1956.
One of only about six double-dwellings at the time of construction, this house rises 1 1/2 stories on a stone foundation that goes deep into the ground to form the walls of a dirt-floored basement. The interior plan of each side of the house is identical with a living room and

kitchen on the first floor and two bedrooms above. *The Washington Post*, October 26, 1962, Section B10.

[92] Document in Jennie Wade file belonging to Mark Nesbitt, Gettysburg, PA.
Deah Schwarzenbach Bruhn told the author in 1991 that her mother, Georgia Schwarzenbach, said that the bullet hole in the original interior door became too large and distorted from tourists probing the hole that it was replaced with a door with "a more authentic-looking hole."

[93] Jennie Wade file at GNMP Library lists songs as: J.P. Webster, "Jenny Wade, the Heroine of Gettysburg," Cleveland, Ohio, 1864-5, words by E.B. Dewing, Esq; "Jenny Wade, the Heroine of Gettysburg," Philadelphia, PA, 1864, words by Albert G. Anderson, dedicated to Major General George G. Meade.

[94] *The Evening Bulletin*, Philadelphia, August 8, 1962.

Index

THOMAS PUBLICATIONS publishes books about the American Colonial era, the Revolutionary War, the Civil War, and other important topics. For a complete list of titles, please write to:

THOMAS PUBLICATIONS
P. O. Box 3031
Gettysburg, PA 17325

Edward F. Guy, Jr. was born in Augusta, Georgia and raised in Belvedere, South Carolina. He earned a Bachelor of fine Arts degree from the University of South Carolina with an emphasis on drawing. Ed has worked as an artist in television, billboards and courtroom sketching before moving to Gettysburg. He came to Gettysburg in 1984 to study the battle and is working as a Licensed Battlefield Guide.

Debra A. Novotny was born in Uniontown, Pennsylvania. She developed an insatiable interest in Civil War history at age 10 from her fifth grade teacher. Debra earned a Bachelor of Science degree in education and a Master's degree in history at California University of Pennsylvania. She has been a Licensed Battlefield Guide since 1975 and has taught American Cultures in the Gettysburg High School for the past eleven years.

Daniel E. Fuhrman was born in 1961 in Hanover, Pennsylvania, where he now lives with his wife, Cynthia S. Roller and their son, Bryce. He graduated from Southwestern High School in 1979, and then studied drafting and design for three years at the Electronics Institute of Harrisburg. Dan is currently employed as a draftsman by P.H. Glatfelter Company of Spring Grove, Pennsylvania. Besides his love of art, he is an avid outdoor enthusiast enjoying sports such as running, biking and racewalking. Fuhrman has now entered college to further his career in art, design and mechanical drawing.

Elizabeth Richwine, of Carlisle, Pennsylvania, received a diploma from the York Academy of Arts after studying commercial art for three years. In her current job, she does freelance work for businesses and private individuals on projects such as logo design; publication design, layout and graphics; architectural renderings and calligraphy work. Although her art projects fill much of her day, "Betsy" finds the time to swim regularly and loves to read. She lives in Carlisle with her husband, Tim, and her children, Benjamin and Laura.